Everything's a Project

Everything's a Project

70 LESSONS FROM SUCCESSFUL PROJECT-DRIVEN ORGANIZATIONS

Ben Snyder

Rock Creek Publishing
12503 E. Euclid Dr., Suite 55
Centennial, CO 80111

Quantity sales. Special discounts are available on quantity purchases by corporations, associations, and others. For details, contact the publisher at the address above.

Library of Congress Control Number: 2011960765
ISBN 978-0-9840404-0-7

Printed in the United States of America

Contents

INTRODUCTION xix

LESSONS

1   Everything's a Project...1

2   Natural Consequences 5

3   Limited Resource Environment 7

4   You Need a Translator on Your Project Team.........................11

5   Haunting Deadlines...15

6   If You Want to Be Relevant, You Need to Innovate..................19

7   Reports of the Project Triangle's Demise are Greatly Exaggerated...........23

8   Stop Parenting Your Staff and Start Coaching Them 25

9   Keep Your Process Pure..29

10 Project-Oriented Skills: Support the Profession and the Role 33

11 Three Traits of People Who Make Things Happen 37

12 Don't Forget About the Project Environment 41

13 Define Your Project into a Box..45

14 Know a Person's Power Base 47

15 Employment's Funny Little Dynamics...51

16 A Project Manager's ROI 55

17 Holding People Accountable 57

18 Your Biggest Project Risk is Poor Project Management 65

19 The Elusive High-Performance Team..69

20 End Users Have Horizon Lines Too..71

21 Four Personas Leaders Must Balance to Be Effective 73

22 Become a Value-Driven Organization...77

23 Estimating: Why We'll Never Get it Right..81

24 The Power of the Question 85

25 Blow it up to Get it Right...89

26 Five Pillars of Practical Project Management 93

27 Three Tactics to Personal Growth..99

28 Great Organizations Reward Prevention, Not Heroism............................103

29 Working With Your Project Triangle's Flexibility 107

30 People Want to Do Good, BUT...111

31 Seven Ground Rules for Every Project Stakeholder...................................115

32 Sometimes the Process is Just as Important as the Product......................119

33 Is Your Project Schedule Dynamic? 123

34 Don't Ask for Permission When Forgiveness is Easier............................127

35 Consistency is the Answer...131

36 How to Pop a Change Bubble...135

37 Three Actions to Ensure Your Vision Becomes a Reality 139

38 The Purpose of V1.0 is to Make a Great V2.0...................................143

39 You are Not the Norm 147

40 Got a Strategy? You Need Portfolio Management...................................151

41 Baselines: A Valuable Tool in Life and Projects 155

42 Was your Project Late or Underestimated? 159

43 When has Documentation Ever Saved Your Butt?...................................161

44 Match Your Medium with Your Message 165

45 The Shortest Path to a Good Project Management Methodology...........169

46 To Confront or Not Confront..173

47 If You Want to Be Efficient, You Need Routine 177

48 Struggling to Define Project Approach?.................................181

49 When Does Done Mean Done?..185

50 Shape Your Organization for Effective Change..........................187

51 Writing Good Requirements...189

52 Get More Out of Life by Seeing the Shades of Gray 193

53 No Problem Can Be Solved Before its Time 197

54 You Can't Manage a Project While Working in it 199

55 So, You Can't Get People to Use the Software Tool....................203

56 Momentum: The X Factor in Project Success 207

57 What You Don't Understand Always Seems Simple....................211

58 Drama Belongs in TV Shows, Not Organizations.......................213

59 Use Metrics to Diagnose Your Project's Ills 217

60 Pruning and Growing Your Team 221

61 Are You an Intentional Leader? 225

62 All Projects Bring about Change...229

63 Why Culture Trumps Your Organization's Proclamations 233

64 Never Care More about Your Project than Your Sponsor Does.............237

65 Four Keys to Building Strong Work Relationships 241

66 Putting Purpose into Your Organization's Efforts.......................245

67 What's the Profile of a Good Project Manager? 249

68 Stop Seeking a Work-Life Balance 253

69 The Chicken or the Egg: Is it the Same for Leaders and Followers? 257

70 When Nice Users Drive You Nuts 261

CONCLUSION...263

Acknowledgements

None of the concepts in this book originated exclusively from me. They arrived through a set of life experiences while working in hundreds of different organizations. They were filtered and constructed through interactions with multiple people in my life. Because of this, I need to acknowledge several individuals and groups.

I want to express gratitude to the clients I have had the privilege of serving in my life. You trusted me and allowed me to enter your organizations and take residence temporarily. While I brought you an expertise, you stretched me and drove me to growth. The scope of this book would not be possible without you.

I am blessed to have people close to me in my life who are strong enough to peel back the layers, look at my behavior, challenge my thinking, and speak their truth to me. You are a gift beyond value. I want to say thank you, from the bottom of my heart, to my Young Presidents Organization forum, the Friday Morning group, and the Systemation team. You have put the concepts in this book through a refining fire.

It is no secret that I have been grammatically challenged since elementary school. I don't spell well at all, my sentence structure sometimes resembles a rope in knots, and my penmanship is closer to impressionist art than English script. This book is appealing to the eye and flows smoothly only because of Laurel Cagan, Systemation's marketing coordinator. Thank you, Laurel, for being patient with me when I corrected my misspelled words with incorrect words the word processor offered me, my tardiness put you under tight deadlines, and I delivered content that needed to be untangled.

Lastly, I want to thank my wife Dawn and kids—Drew, Audra, and Reid. You love me unconditionally, and that has fueled my aspirations, giving me the strength to embrace uncertainty. You have kept me grounded with your ever-present observations and blunt confrontations. I'm grateful for it and wouldn't have it any other way. I love you all.

Introduction

M ost organizational leaders say they're compensated for executing a strategy and maintaining daily operations. While true, this is an overly glorified way to describe their jobs. Stated bluntly, leaders from the C-level down to line managers are responsible for accomplishing, producing, innovating, and providing value for their organizations; you know, doing good things and getting work done. Their bonuses and annual pay increases are tied to how well they perform these tasks.

Getting work done sounds simplistic, but it's actually very demanding. By definition, leaders do little of the work, and instead rely on others to get it done. That means these leaders are more focused on orchestrating than performing. They may have succeeded in the past based on how well they did the work, but the rules for success have changed. Now, they lead the people who do the work. In addition, their scope of responsibility has broadened; they're now pulled in many different directions. Leaders don't always know what they don't know, but they will soon enough, because it will knock them upside the head when they least expect it. Sounds like a lot of fun, eh? Actually, getting work done can be very rewarding with just a little structure for focusing a leader's attention, exploration, and energy.

So, how does work get done? It gets done through **people, projects, and organizations**. Today, there are a lot of topics under these three major categories that make a leader's job demanding. Knowing them provides the leader with a map for getting more work done that's of higher quality. Let's take a look at these three categories in further detail.

People

People are the most prevalent resource in companies, and they're our most complex resource. People are highly unique, each with different strengths and weaknesses, not to mention likes and dislikes. There's no "one size fits all" when you engage and interact with them. People are also very dynamic; they can change from year to year or hour to hour based on circumstances.

Finding the right person for an open position is a mixture of science and intuition. Often, you have to kiss a few frogs before you find your prince. Finding the prince puts you on the path to good production, but being handicapped with the wrong frog affects the quality of everyone's work.

Helping people work better together has a lot to do with helping them relate well with one another. It starts with leaders relating to their subordinates, then continues to everyone else. If people in a department don't learn to play well in the sandbox together, energy is diverted away from production to individual survival and settling scores.

Managing performance is both proactive and reactive. Leaders must learn what motivates individuals and act on it. They must ensure that the training individuals need keeps up with what the organization needs, and look for teachable moments. Coaching and mentoring are required to help individuals boost their performance to the next level. Someone who reaches a plateau will see their value to the organization deteriorate over time. So, as you will discover while you read this book, leaders must invest the energy to keep high performers producing high value. This will minimize employee turnover and save the organization energy, time, and money.

Projects

Projects are the mechanism we use to move our departments forward one step at a time. Projects are what we use to execute our initiatives in chunks, make our products better, organize our efforts, and turn "what could be" into "what is." In reality, everything is a project. Some are big. Some are small. Some require a lot of process and discipline, while others can be handled on the fly. There's a very specific set of skills and processes that are required to get work done through projects effectively and consistently.

Fleshing out the details of what needs to be accomplished keeps the horse before the cart. For some reason, we're more interested in how to design and build something than in what we need to build. Many a project has failed because of this.

Matching the right approach for producing a product with the specific product being produced can be difficult. To make sure the approach is aligned with the product, asking these three questions may be necessary:

1. Is the product something you produce all the time or is it highly unique?

2. Can the end result be easily envisioned or must the customer interact with it and give feedback many times before the product is complete?
3. Are the risks involved minimal or must we prove that critical pieces are feasible before we invest heavily in production?

All these factors influence the approach you take and can affect the efficiency of your projects.

Managing the efforts of all project resources makes the project more predictable. That means finishing the project on time so it integrates with other co-dependent projects, staying within budget so the project does not have to steal funds from future projects, and freeing up people when other projects are expecting them to be added. Without predictability, all projects being worked on concurrently, as well as those projected to start in the future, are at risk.

Organizations

Organizations provide the environment for people and projects. They are an ecosystem for healthy effort and production. When organizations are at their best, they are hardly noticed. At their worst, they can be as restrictive as shackles and toxic as an oil spill. Organizations can create an emotional tie with people by making them feel comfortable and wanted, or threatened, pushing them to a "fight or flight" response.

An organization's culture helps you to know what to expect from the environment, and provides guidance when you're operating in an unpredictable, "gray area." This is huge, considering we spend a lot of emotional energy shielding ourselves from unpredictable situations. There are many more gray areas than situations that are black and white.

A reasonable governance system is needed in organizations to bring about order and reap economies of scale.. Policies and procedures are not bad; people often appreciate them when they're appropriate, and thus ensure stability and guarantee justice. When policies are not appropriate, they can incite people to game the system through sleight of hand, deception, or outright rebellion.

Organizations have to provide a purpose and vision so individuals feel a sense of community and belonging. This helps them feel that their individual efforts are magnified when they're combined with those of others, and that they're contributing to something bigger and better that will make a difference. When a purpose and vision are clear, work takes on a special value that's worth the extra effort and sacrifice. Without purpose and vision, narcissism creeps in and destroys community. Work becomes just work, with no intrinsic value.

Organizations that understand that the majority of their work is accomplished through projects and that paying attention to human interaction, project skills, and organizational influences dramatically affects project performance, and thus organizational performance are called project-driven organizations. These are the organizations that have stepped their game up and have gotten noticed in the last decade.

Maturing as a project-driven organization requires input in the form of best practices, experience in trying new approaches, and sharing lessons learned that prevent the organization from making the same mistake again. This book is a collection of lessons learned over many years that come from people, projects, and organizations. The advice offered is practical in nature and focused more on the art than the science of getting the most out of people and producing greater project results.

Who Should Read this Book?

The content in this book is extremely relevant to the realities of today's organizations that are being forced to produce more than they did five years ago with fewer employees and resources. The low-hanging fruit of efficiencies have been harvested; now it's time for organizations to take what they have, look at things from a different perspective, and get better—incrementally—at producing results.

This book is written for executives and managers who find themselves in this type of situation. Their organizations may be very aware that projects are the vehicle for getting work done, or they're just becoming aware of that. For those working in **"very aware" organizations,** there are lessons that will appeal to both beginning and advanced individuals. For those in **"newly aware" organizations**, there are enough basic lessons to provide a foundation in managing projects, to which they can add more advanced lessons. In many chapters, actual examples of work-related situations are used to illustrate the points made. *(The names used in those examples are not the real names of the people involved.)*

How to Use This Book

R eaders can move through this book sequentially, or jump around and select lessons that pique their interests. *(If you want to jump around, follow the guide below that categorizes each chapter.)* Either way, the goal of this book is to help readers and their organizations work more effectively.

Lessons about People

2   Natural Consequences 5

5   Haunting Deadlines...15

11 Three Traits of People who Make Things Happen 37

14 Know a Person's Power Base..47

17 Holding People Accountable 57

21 Four Personas Leaders Must Balance to be Effective.....................73

24 The Power of the Question 85

27 Three Tactics to Personal Growth 99

30 People Want to do Good, BUT... 111

32 Sometimes the Process is Just as Important as the Product....................119

34 Don't ask for Permission When Forgiveness is Easier................................127

36 How to Pop a Change Bubble 135

39 You are not the Norm 147

44 Match Your Medium With Your Message 165

46 To Confront or Not Confront...173

52 Get More out of Life by Seeing the Shades of Gray....................193

57 What you Don't Understand Always Seems Simple....................211

60 Pruning and Growing Your Team 221

65 Four Keys to Building Strong Work Relationships 241

68 Stop Seeking a Work-Life Balance 253

70 When Nice Users Drive you Nuts 261

Lessons about Projects

1 Everything's a Project..1

4 You Need a Translator on Your Project Team................................11

7 Reports of the Project Triangle's Demise are Greatly Exaggerated............23

10 Project-Oriented Skills: Support the Profession and the Role 33

13 Define Your Project Into a Box 45

16 A Project Manager's ROI 55

18 Your Biggest Project Risk is Poor Project Management................................65

20 End Users Have Horizon Lines Too..................................71

23 Estimating: Why We'll Never get it Right.............................81

26 Five Pillars of Practical Project Management.............................93

29 Working With Your Project Triangle's Flexibility 107

31 Seven Ground Rules for Every Project Stakeholder....................115

33 Is Your Project Schedule Dynamic? 123

38 The Purpose of V1.0 is to Make a Great V2.0..........................143

41   Baselines: A Valuable Tool in Life and Projects 155

42   Was your Project Late or Underestimated? 159

43   When has Documentation Ever Saved Your Butt? 161

45   The Shortest Path to a Good Project Management Methodology 169

48   Struggling to Define Project Approach? 181

49   When Does Done Mean Done? 185

51   Writing Good Requirements 189

54   You Can't Manage a Project While Working in it 199

56   Momentum: The X Factor in Project Success 207

59   Use Metrics to Diagnose Your Project's Ills 217

62   All Projects Bring About Change 229

64   Never Care More About Your Project Than Your Sponsor Does 237

67   What's the Profile of a Good Project Manager? 249

Lessons About Organizations

3   Limited Resource Environment 7

6   If you Want to be Relevant, You need to Innovate 19

8 Stop Parenting Your Staff and Start Coaching Them 25

9 Keep Your Process Pure..29

12 Don't Forget About the Project Environment 41

15 Employment's Funny Little Dynamics...51

19 The Elusive High-Performance Team..69

22 Become a Value-Driven Organization...77

25 Blow it up to get it Right 89

28 Great Organizations Reward Prevention, Not Heroism..............................103

35 Consistency is the Answer..131

37 Three Actions to Ensure Your Vision Becomes a Reality 139

40 Got a Strategy? You Need Portfolio Management......................................151

47 If you Want to be Efficient, you Need Routine 177

50 Shape Your Organization for Effective Change..187

53 No Problem can be Solved Before its Time...197

55 So, you Can't get People to Use the Software Tool....................................203

58 Drama Belongs in TV Shows, Not Organizations 213

61 Are you an Intentional Leader? 225

63   Why Culture Trumps Your Organization's Proclamations 233

66   Putting Purpose Into Your Organization's Efforts 245

69   The Chicken or the Egg: Is it the Same for Leaders and Followers? 257

Everything's a Project

Lesson 1

Everything's a Project

The Industrial Revolution brought about the division of labor, repeatable tasks, factories, and assembly lines. Work was accomplished by people whose perspectives were only as broad as the tasks they were assigned. A strong and rigid hierarchy of management kept all the people in line and all the pieces together. The process and outcome were simple and repeatable.

In the 1980s, knowledge workers began to emerge in the workforce with specialized skills that were not developed by experience—as in the past—but by learning. Because of the degree of their specialization, knowledge workers required less management and more autonomy, thus beginning the "softening" of management's heavy-handedness.

Then came the quality movement, in which problems tended to require cross-departmental groups of individuals to solve them. This led to the team explosion in the early 1990s. The goal of this movement was high performance through clear objectives and self-direction, via collaboration.

Amid the rise in knowledge workers and the increase in work being accomplished through teams, projects emerged. Even though projects have been around since the Pharaohs of Egypt, this unique combination of events led to an increased awareness and explosion of projects in the mid-1990s.

But not all organizations embraced this evolution at the same speed. Science—and technology—oriented markets tended to embrace it faster. Today, all industries and organizations are at a state in which all work gets done through projects.

A project is a temporary endeavor undertaken to create a unique product or service, either **temporary**, meaning every project has a definite beginning and a definite end, or **unique**, meaning the product or service is different in some distinguishing way from other similar products or services.

Projects are everywhere. We may not always see them because of their simplicity or scale, but by definition they are there. Take for example, a child's birthday party, a family reunion, or a vacation. They're all unique and temporary endeavors. While these examples may not appear on your radar screen of concern, the following business projects might:

- **Departmental initiatives:** Installing an enterprise resource planning (ERP) system, developing a marketing campaign, or resolving a Six Sigma process anomaly.
- **Product development:** Designing a better machine, inventing a new Post-it® note, or making a better tasting non-fat ice cream.
- **Mergers and acquisitions:** Merging two car companies. Purchasing a new drug formulation, bringing it through four phases of testing, and introducing it to the market. Or, acquiring smaller lending institutions and merging them into an existing institution.
- **Conferences and functions:** Putting on an internal sales conference, hosting heads of state, or organizing a non-profit fundraiser.

- **Administrative activities:** Creating year-end financial reports, completing requests for proposals, or planning and coordinating office moves.

While all work in today's world gets done through projects, not all organizations label them projects, and therefore take advantage of the well-developed project disciplines available to organizations. Without project management, business analysis, and portfolio management disciplines, projects have less chance of success. And without them, project sponsors, team members, and project benefactors get frustrated because of incomplete visions, lack of organization, wasted efforts, and constant delays.

Projects are here to stay, and so is the need to work more efficiently and effectively. Market demands and global competition are going to keep the pressure on organizations, so it's time to recognize projects —big and small—for what they are and embrace the disciplines associated with them. It's time to change and get better.

Lesson 2

Natural Consequences

All of us have heard at some time in our lives, "If you don't do _____ (fill in the blank) there will be consequences." Sometimes we did what we were supposed to do and avoided the consequences. Other times, we didn't fare so well. Consequences are life's little learning agents. But did you know there are such things as natural consequences and unnatural consequences?

In the working world, **natural consequences** flow out of an employee knowing what behavior is expected and why it's expected (the intent). If they behave contrarily and it causes a negative result, the consequence should be related to rectifying the negative result. This way, the consequence emphasizes the importance of the expectation. This is when learning happens. Let me give you an example:

Four people on a project team have a task due on Friday and all four of the tasks must be completed for the product implementation to start Monday. The desired behavior is for them to finish their tasks by the agreed-upon deadline. The reason for this expectation is so the product implementation is completed on time. Jim did not finish his task Friday. A natural consequence would be to have Jim work the weekend to complete the task before Monday morning. The consequence is directly related to the

intent of the expectation. The message Jim hears is that if a task needs
to get done on time to keep the project on time, then get it done.

Unnatural consequences occur when the consequence does not relate to the intent of the expected behavior. This can happen when the intent of the expected behavior is known but the wrong consequence is selected. Or, the intent of the expected behavior is not known and any chosen consequence would not relate to it. As a result, there is no learning, and the consequence comes off as being punitive on the manager's part. Here's an example of an unnatural consequence:

Susan travels every so often on company business. She has a history of
slightly bending the travel policies. After her last trip, she submitted her
expenses and it was revealed that she rented a luxury car instead of
mid-size car. The manager was upset and decided to not allow Susan
to go on vacation at the end of the month. This is an unnatural conse-
quence. The consequence has nothing to do with why there are company
travel policies. The company has travel policies to prevent it from paying
frivolous expenses, and the only thing this consequence emphasized was
that the manager was upset and wanted to punish Susan.

A natural consequence would be to not refund Susan for her rental car expense. The message Susan would hear is that, when on company travel, keep the expenses in line with the travel policies and don't waste the company's money.

We all want people to learn from their poor decisions or behavior. Help them learn by using natural consequences. That also keeps you from unnecessarily putting yourself in the doghouse.

Lesson 3

Limited Resource Environment

All organizations operate in a limited resource environment. There is always more work that can be done than there are resources to do it. And, given our current economic conditions, this is even truer today. Denying or ignoring this fact sets off a chain reaction in organizations.

Executives at the top need better business results, so they lean on mid-level managers to produce more. Mid-level managers say "yes" to more projects because they don't want to appear unresponsive to business needs. These decisions then lead to more projects being launched which, in turn, create more work demands for folks who actually do the work.

With this, projects start slipping because people in the trenches have too much to do. Then pressure comes from on high, and of course, the "squeaky wheel" projects get the grease. Not that the squeaky wheels are the highest-priority projects; they're the loudest or most noticed. So, now, there's a good chance the projects with the highest potential to bring about business results are receiving the least attention. It's madness.

In this situation, there are only three options for organizations: Hire more resources, make the current resources more efficient, or launch fewer projects. As I said earlier, there is always more work that can be done and, if acquiring more resources were an option, most organizations would have hired them already. That leaves us with either becoming more efficient in the way employees work, or working on fewer projects.

Inside every manager is some level of belief that their employees are not working as hard as they can. Some are very trusting of their employees but still have this thought in the back of their minds, even if that thought is very small. Some managers are very distrusting, and are convinced their employees are sandbagging. But no one really knows the truth; they're guided only by intuition. Pushing employees beyond what they say they can accomplish within a specified period of time is one way to increase efficiency, but it's exactly what brings on the madness I described above.

A better way to increase efficiency is to invest in skills training and engage in process improvement initiatives. Yes, this will cause efficiency to decrease at first, but then you'll reap the rewards and surge past the point from which you started. Regardless, if you don't do anything, you can't magically think greater efficiencies will appear.

You may feel as if you're falling behind when you decide to work on fewer projects. You know what needs to be accomplished to make your company more competitive, and if you can't do it, you feel as though you're going to lose the fight. While these feelings are real, the end result is never that dramatic. Take the time to **prioritize the importance of each project against your strategic plans**. First, number them 1, 2, 3, 4, and so on. Next, start with the highest priority project and then add the next-highest priority, making sure you get buy-in on what work can be accomplished during that time frame. Then, when you reach your work capacity limit, draw a line and stop adding projects until you gain more capacity. Employees will feel better and be more capable of surges in effort when they must make a deadline.

The symptoms of exceeding the capacity of your resources are easy to see; however, fixing the problem is hard to do. It requires restraint and investment. No one said management is easy.

Lesson 4

You Need a Translator on Your Project Team

All projects have one thing in common: a communication gap between the visionary and the creator. The visionary comes in many forms. They may be an innovator, a department head, or a line of business. They are the ones who determine the scope of a project. Creators come in many forms too: small teams, whole organizations, or an individual. They take the scope as defined by the visionary and complete the required work to make it a reality.

Visionaries and creators are two different parties. They have different roles in their organizations, and different skill sets. They're different in how they view their environments and approach their work. Because of this, there's a communication gap between the two groups.

When it comes to projects, the communication gap results in products or deliverables being produced by the creators that don't match the visionaries' intent. That leads to countless hours of rework or do-overs, resulting in blown budgets and time delays. Here's an example of a communication gap:

Matt (the visionary) found himself in this situation when he contracted with a company to overhaul his landscaping. He met with the owner of the landscaping company (the creator) for eight hours and explained what he was envisioning. The owner quoted a price and timetable. Matt gave his OK and work began the following month. Two-thirds of the way through the project Matt, to his dismay, began seeing the finished product. Yes there were pathways, trees, shrubs, grass, a waterfall, and a gazebo, but they were not what he had envisioned. Instead of curved pathways, they were straight. Instead of a mixture of tall and short bushes, all were the same height, and instead of the waterfall having four falls, there were only two. Work stopped, meetings were conducted, more money was requested and when they were all finished it was the middle of fall instead of summer.

This is where the role of a **translator** comes in. Professional translators bridge communication gaps by knowing both parties' lingo and understanding their unique cultures, and are able to express both the verbal and non-verbal components of a message. Translators on project teams are those who understand both the world of the visionary and of the creator. They have knowledge that aids them in taking the visionary's message and expressing it to the creator through different means so they understand the original intent. Translators also communicate the cold details, such as what color or size of type to use, as well as the warm impressions of what they see.

In the software industry, the role of the translator has been formalized into the business analyst (BA), who uses a whole suite of processes and tools to succeed. The following story illustrates this nicely:

Alexis was the point person for a small group of her peers in her company's customer service center. To date, the company had very few technology-enabled tools to do their jobs. Money had been set aside for a project to develop a system that would allow them to better serve their customers. When it was time to start the project the company's IT department assigned a business analyst to their project team. The BA held multiple meetings with Alexis and her team. Then the BA produced several documents and diagrams for their review. Alexis was surprised by the level of detail and determination the BA showed in making sure every nuance of the final product's nature was addressed. In fact, at times it became annoying to her since she just wanted the IT department to start working on the project. But, when all was said and done, the end product replicated all of Alexis's and her team's vision for their customer-support tool.

Translators have a unique role during projects. Many project leaders try to satisfy this role themselves or pass it on to a less than capable person. This is not a good idea since it's not about just knowing the lingo of both parties. Understanding both the visionary and creator environments, and noticing the spoken and unspoken components of a message are equally important. Plus, the wider the communication gap, the more experienced a translator you need.

On your next project, pay attention to how big the communications gap is between the visionary and your team. The bigger the gap the harder you'll have to work to find the right translator. It's like being overseas: You don't want to think you're ordering chicken and find out you ordered the rat eyes.

Lesson 5

Haunting Deadlines

W orking on projects can be very demanding, taxing our energy and resiliency. There are often spurts of overtime that have to be put in to get a project back on track. Sometimes you have to work months upon months of long hours just to stay only a little behind. If you work on just one project at a time, you might catch a break. However, most people these days seem to be working on *multiple* projects at any given time.

There has been a lot published on the effects of working overtime for prolonged periods. Researchers have determined that only bursts of overtime – such as, 50 hours a week for three weeks – are effective. Dr. Jim Loehr of the Human Performance Institute talks about viewing effort at work like making waves. You have to make time for breaks so you can be more effective when you're working. While this sounds easy, it's hard to put into practice. Thankfully, companies have instituted policies for holidays and vacations that allow us to get away from our work environments and enjoy doing other things or nothing at all.

Vacations and holidays take care of the physical and mental effects of working long hours, but what about the emotional effects of constantly chasing deadlines? Deadlines are points in time that were negotiated in the past and are not changed easily. When we're on holiday or vacation, deadlines don't simply go away and they don't care if we've taken time off.

Deadlines can be a source of accomplishment if they don't overwhelm you. However, this is not the case for most folks. Deadlines are a major source of stress that distract us and take us away from our family and friends. Those of you who are working on multiple projects know that they haunt you, even to the point of disrupting your sleep and causing nightmares. Six to 12 months of constantly challenging deadlines can drain and numb you emotionally, potentially resulting in depression and mood swings.

Unfortunately, deadlines are a core component of projects. They have to exist to facilitate completing the project at an expected point in time. Deadlines are not going to go away. The solution to them? Learn how to minimize their emotional toll. For example:

Joe noticed his project team was getting overly stressed toward the end of a nine-month stretch of continuously tight deadlines. Some members were getting very thin on patience. Others were becoming prone to emotional outbursts. Joe knew he was driving his team members pretty hard and forced each of them to take a one-week vacation. When they returned, he noticed that they were still stressed.

After a significant emotional outburst in a meeting by one of his team members, Joe called a time out and told his team to go back to their desks and write down five work-related things they have wanted to do but have not had time for because of the constant deadlines. He then instructed them to start doing the things on their list and stop working on the project altogether for one week. He then contacted his department head and negotiated two-week extensions for all deadlines. After the one-week break, the team began work on the project with a new emotional disposition. They completed the project over the next three months without missing a deadline.

Joe's story is a great example of how to mitigate the emotional stress of haunting deadlines. The key to his success was to unconditionally slip the deadlines. This gave his team a tangible sign to release the stress they were carrying. This could have been combined with a one-week vacation, but it seems to produce better results if team members stay at work and do something they've been *wanting* to do. Usually, this includes researching tools that would help them become more efficient, or gaining knowledge that would help them be more effective.

Everyone handles the stress of constant deadlines differently. That means everyone has to be aware of their own emotional state and take steps to keep themselves from going over the edge. That being said, it helps to have a manager who is aware and looks out for the welfare of his team members, as well as the project deadlines.

Lesson 6

If You Want to Be Relevant, You Need to Innovate

In today's environment, relevance is a matter of survival. Having a relevant organization means being pertinent, connected, or applicable to your company or industry. It means being current, not out of date when it comes to the latest practices, and having a very strong value proposition for your internal or external clients. Organizations that are not relevant have become complacent or lazy and either unable or slow to change. They're obsolete and destined for outsourcing or extinction.

We've seen numerous organizations on this path, such as Blockbuster, Palm, AOL, and newspaper companies. Even the Arlington National Cemetery fell to this problem after the public found out it had misidentified hundreds of buried remains. Separate investigations pointed to the lack of established policies and procedures, a failure to automate records, and long-term systemic problems. Thankfully, we have also seen many other organizations overcome obsolescence and remain relevant, notably Napster, Netflix, Google, and Facebook.

If you want to be relevant, you need to innovate. When people think of innovation, they think of big market disrupters that are totally new and fresh with lots of pizzazz. But in organizations seeking relevance, this is not the case. Innovation is incremental improvements, unique ways of doing the same thing, and performing the same function but with a different set of problems.

OK, you get that you need to be innovative, but you want to know how to take your first steps toward it. The most important first step is realizing that innovation cannot be commanded, it must grow out of a favorable environment. Variances in actions, style, and attitude must be allowed for innovation to flourish. Let me give you an example of how important this is:

> *Everyone knows that Singapore's cities are meticulously clean with safe streets, minimal congestion, and well-behaved citizens. Government officials are very proud of this, but back in the late 1990s they recognized their cities lacked spontaneity and artistic creativity. So, they launched a campaign to audition and hire street performers. Then, they let actors, jugglers, and musicians who played American folk songs play on the streets. But because of restrictive government policy that dictated what they could do, this campaign did little to boost their cities' creativity and innovation. The government didn't realize that it was overseeing a different society that did not foster individual freedom, unlike the U.S.*

Here are five specifics that will help you create an environment that allows variances in action, style, and attitude:

1. **As a leader, you need to get uncomfortable.** You need to exert less control and encourage employees to push the norms. There should be much less focus on avoiding failure and more on trying new things. Tell employees what you want and then let them get it done in their own unique ways. Grow a thicker skin and encourage employees to openly challenge you.

2. **Make sure some of your key employees love change.** This can be tested for with psychological assessments such as Myers-Briggs. These employees will welcome change for change sake and will come up with lots of ways things should

be different. The employees can be hard to manage because you have to give these employees room for their ideas. Just be sure that the organization adheres to its core mission. If you don't have employees who will welcome change, find them. It's critical.

3.   **Look for things your organization seems to hold onto because they're easy or require no effort to retain.** Confront people who nay-say ideas because they have been tried before. Ask how your organization can do things differently even if they're not necessarily broken. Pick something randomly and ask your staff to change it and make it better.

4.   **Play with new technology even if you don't have a need for it.** Allow employees time to think, ponder, and conduct "what if" experiments. Make sure everyone is an expert at searching Google. Bring in experts from other companies, inside and outside your industry, to talk about what they do. This will add fuel for your innovation opportunities.

5.   **Get close to your internal or external clients.** Fully understand their environments and the day-to-day issues they encounter. Don't focus only on the areas of their organizations you contribute to. This is where you can find special ways to help them get better. See if they will let you sit with them for a day. (They can call it "Take your provider to work day.")

There's no other path to becoming and remaining relevant. If you want your organization to have an extremely powerful value proposition, you have to innovate. This is not easy and will not happen overnight. Most importantly, it requires you, as a leader, to change in order to create change in your organization.

Lesson 7

Reports of the Project Triangle's Demise are Greatly Exaggerated

The theorists have won. The fourth edition of the Project Management Institute's (PMI) Project Management Body of Knowledge (PMBOK) has done away with the project triangle, often referred to as the triple constraint. For more than 50 years, this simple model allowed people inside and outside the project management profession to understand the high-level dynamics involved in projects.

The project triangle represents the relationships between scope, time, and cost. **Scope** is the sum of all products and services to be provided. It includes all the work that must be performed to deliver the product or service (tasks and activities) at the negotiated grade (level of quality and amount of redundancy). **Time** is the duration that is needed to complete all the associated project work (calendar days, months, and years). **Cost** is the monetary value of the labor expended and all other direct charges that will be incurred during the project (travel, hardware, and software).

When the value of one side is changed, one or both of the other sides are almost always affected. Successfully managing projects requires an understanding of the dynamics of these relationships. When one side of the triangle is an accurate reflection of the demands of the other two sides, the project triangle is said to be harmonized. For example, a project with a scope of building a 5,000-square-foot home in two months at a cost of $40,000 is unrealistic; time does not accurately represent the demands of scope and cost. To harmonize the triangular relationship of this project, the cost of the home would have to be increased or its scope decreased, or both.

Boo-yah! That's it! This straightforward concept has allowed numerous project managers, project sponsors, and team members to come together and work through project issues. PMI has replaced the project triangle with an infinite number of constraints, such as time, cost, and risks. While the change is not wrong, it provides no practical utility.

PMI may not recognize the project triangle anymore, but it's still a good thing to have in your tool belt.

Lesson 8

Stop Parenting Your Staff and Start Coaching Them

I t's very natural for parents to take responsibility for their children. At a young age, kids don't know how to be responsible for themselves, but the goal of every parent is to slowly show and allow their children to be responsible for themselves. Certainly, after one becomes 18 they *should* be mostly responsible for themselves. Upon being hired for a professional job they *most definitely* should be fully responsible.

Unfortunately, this is not always the case. Most managers at some point in their careers have encountered individuals or groups of employees who make them feel as though they're running an adult day care facility.

The fact is, individual employees alone are responsible for having the required knowledge and skills to fulfill their job descriptions, understanding the context associated with them, making good decisions while fulfilling their jobs, and performing well within their scope. In all these areas, employees are responsible for initiating and obtaining what they lack. Managers may choose to help them, but ultimately, it's the employee's responsibility.

However, sometimes the environment of an organization doesn't allow for growth in its employees. Some managers are acutely distrusting of employees' ability to make decisions and perform at a specific level of competence. They hover over employees, giving direction and monitoring their actions. Some managers like this because it puts them in the powerful position of being the expert who knows everything and the supervisor of underlings who know nothing. In fact, they may specifically hire people too junior for a position so that they will never be threatened. Again, some managers enjoy this type of relationship with their employees, but can, at times, become overwhelmed and angry at having to give direction constantly.

Then, there are the employees who play helpless and seduce managers into constantly intervening in their work, giving direction, and acting as their quality control function. They don't want to be empowered and take responsibility; they want to be followers. Employees exhibit another childish behavior when they screw up and want someone to rescue them from a situation. Often, they will manipulate others to take over the crises and fix their problems.

Managers carry at least 50% of the blame for these bad behaviors. Either they instigate the bad behavior with their actions or they allow employees to get away with not taking responsibility. The best way for you, the manager, to change this behavior is to learn to play the role of a professional coach. Follow these four pieces of advice:

1. **The focus within the organization should never be on you; it should be about your organization, department, or project and its performance.** This is what coaches do. They focus on creating the best environment for their players to succeed. They find the best talent and could care less if the players perform better than he ever could. Coaches realize they cannot play in the game and must let their players do so without constant intervention. They look for teachable moments from the bench to help players get better.

2. **Don't let employees get addicted to your constant help and guidance.** It would be unthinkable for a player to constantly seek direction and approval from the coach while in a game. Coaches would get rid of any player who did. Managers

should wean employees from this behavior by forcing them to work independently.

Example: Susan was responsible for putting on the department's yearly dinner. She got the menu from the high-end restaurant and needed to select a family-style offering for the employees to choose from. She was scared to make the decision on her own and repeatedly asked her manager for help. He told her the decision was hers and that people would enjoy anything she picked. Then she started asking the employees what they wanted and there was no consensus. Finally, her manager sent an email telling people that Susan needed to make the decision on her own and not to help her anymore. With the deadline approaching, she reluctantly chose the items from the menu. People loved the food, and the dinner was a success.

3. **Don't rescue employees from predicaments they get themselves into.** You may know the best way to get out of the situation while incurring the least amount of pain, but if you rescue them they will avoid the sting that makes sure they never do it again.

Example: Alex was notorious for promising things to clients and putting the operations team in a bind to meet them. Finally, the VP of operations, Becky, got fed up and told Alex and his manager they were not going to be rescued anymore. In one situation, Alex and his manager pleaded with Becky for help since a major client would be very upset if things were not delivered as promised. Becky told them it was always a major client and her team in the past had always felt manipulated into making it right for them. From now on her organization would not rescue Alex. He was the one who promised it and he needed to work it out with the client. Operations never had this problem with Alex again.

4. **Help your employees only as much as they help themselves.** Coaches help players only when players take the initiative to help themselves; they have to be coachable to receive any attention. Players who resist external input and don't strive to get better get cut from the team.

Example: Wil was always below the mean when it came to his performance. As a result, he received little to no raise in each of the previous three years. Wil finally decided to meet with his manager, Reid, and asked how he could get better. Reid told him the areas he could improve, but Wil then asked for exact steps and actions. This meant Wil would never get better in the future because he couldn't figure it out for himself. Reid told Wil to figure it out, as had the top performers in his organization. Wil never improved and was eventually let go.

Shifting from a manager who parents their employees to a coach is very difficult. It's best accomplished with group support, encouragement, and advice. Role playing and reviewing past situations in the group is invaluable. It could take a few years to make the transition depending how deep you are into parenting your employees (which actually isn't that long if you plan to be in management the rest of your life). So, find or put together a group and make it happen. It's your responsibility.

Lesson 9

Keep Your Process Pure

N o one needs to beat the drum about the importance of processes in business. Processes have been a valuable tool since the
start of the Industrial Revolution as a way to establish uniformity and
gain efficiencies. Some processes are documented into formal procedures. Others remain informal but are still commonly understood.
Most processes are composed of action steps with strategically placed
gate points to obtain consensus or establish authority for moving forward. Pure processes are true to their intent, serve only one function,
and require the least effort while providing the most value. Processes
that become contaminated usually do so in two different ways: by
trying to **accommodate all possible situations** and attempting to
control malicious participants.

Processes that Accommodate All Possible Situations

Processes are usually designed to accommodate about 90% of situations that occur. When an extremely rare situation presents itself and
leads to a negative result, management will be tempted to change the
process to handle the rare situation when it occurs again (regardless of

the impact on the process). The extra effort that is imposed to cover an extremely rare situation usually has no payoff. Furthermore, all processes have inherent risk but most of the risk is never encountered and, rightly so, is off our radar screen of concern. Just because we encounter a risk doesn't mean we should track it on our radar forever.

Processes that Try to Control Malicious Participants

Sometimes individuals feel they have special needs that compel them to deviate from the defined processes. It may be to avoid a gate point or to leverage a loophole so the individual can have greater access to resources for their personal gain, such as expediting a purchase order ahead of others without permission. These deviations may or may not go unnoticed. But when they're noticed, management always wants to include additional steps or gate points to ensure these abuses don't occur in the future. The addition of gate points due to one person's actions is commonly known as "tyranny of the minority." When this occurs, everyone has to expend additional time and effort on the process just because of the actions of one individual.

The best thing to do in this case is to address the behavior of the rogue individual. They will often play victim when confronted, saying they didn't know better or didn't understand the situation, but don't hesitate or withdraw from your position. If the majority can follow the process, then the rogue individual can too. It's up to him or her to learn the right way and how to stick to it.

Regardless of how they came to be, these appendages to the original processes are usually unjustified, stay past their need, and end up being followed blindly, wasting people's effort and time. They diminish the value of the process and cause frustration.

Let's take Alice for example. She's the manager of a systems engineering organization and her department is responsible for the integration of various spacecraft subsystems. Because these subsystems are being built in different parts of the country, Alice's team travels extensively. Her company has travel guidelines but because her department is currently over budget, she has been keeping a close eye on travel expenditures. Over time, Alice began to realize that one of her employees, Tim, was constantly working outside the guidelines. He always had excuses and Alice had been struggling with how to rein him in. At her wits' end, Alice decided to add an additional gate point in the travel procedure that required everyone to get authority from her before they deviated from the guidelines. This action did stop Tim from abusing the guidelines, but it also caused everyone else on her team (who were not abusing the guidelines) to take extra effort and time to get approval for unique situations they typically dealt with on their own. In one situation, Jennifer, another employee, could not get authority to change her air travel plans to come home early because Alice was out sick. This resulted in additional lodging costs since Jennifer had to stay two days longer than needed, not to mention a loss of productivity from being away from the office unnecessarily.

In your organization, fight for pure process and procedures. Make it a personal campaign. It will mean moving away from a controlling mindset and toward personal responsibility. It will also mean moving away from risk aversion and toward embracing ambiguity. While doing this may be hard, the end result will be a much more efficient organization.

Lesson 10

Project-Oriented Skills:
Support the Profession and the Role

M any job fields have professional designations; doctors, lawyers, accountants, Realtors, etc. The same goes for project-oriented skills. The Project Management Institute certifies project managers, The International Institute for Business Analysis certifies business analysts, and The Scrum Alliance certifies agile developers. The organizations that certify these professions have standards that define in great detail all the terminology, processes, and skills for their disciplines; the best practices the experts must know.

These professional designations are a means of separating those who have the expertise from those who don't. Companies often invest heavily to have their employees trained and certified in different professions to establish a standard for professional development or to establish credibility in the workplace and in the market.

On medium—and large—size project teams, it's not unusual to find multiple individuals with one or more of these designations because larger projects are critical to a business's success and are very costly. Having certified professionals on these large project teams gives the project a much better chance of producing the desired results. For companies, the return on investment to develop employees and get them certified is definitely warranted.

What about smaller projects that don't require certified profession-als but do require individuals to perform the roles of those profes-sions? As you know, organizations have many more small projects than medium to large ones. That means there are lots of project leaders on these smaller projects with the responsibility of all three roles (project management, requirements management, and iterative development) residing squarely on their backs; however, these sturdy individuals don't always get the support they need to perform better. The biggest reason for this is that unless you're pursuing an expertise in something, your efforts are not considered worthy of attention or investment.

Organizations can't afford to continue with this mindset as work trends indicate an increase in smaller projects in the future. Project management, requirements management, and iterative development roles in these projects will need management's attention and support. To support these project leads in their roles, a methodology has to be developed, training needs must be provided, and expectations need to be set. Let's look at each of these areas of support.

The methodology that needs to be developed can't look exactly like the one certified professionals are already using. This will only overwhelm project leads and send them running for the hills. Consider the following four things when developing a joint role methodology. It has to be:

1. **Referable**: It has some relationship to the formal professions. A common lingo helps accelerate the maturation process up and down the organization.
2. **Malleable**: It blends all three roles (project management, requirements management, and iterative development) into one. The certified professionals have very distinct boundaries between them that cause confusion. This has to be avoided.
3. **Congruent**: It aligns with the individual's natural work style. Most non–certified professionals have a different work style

based on their level and function. It's best to err on the less formal side of things.

4. **Practical**: It's easily applied in the real world. If it's going to be accepted and followed, it has to be valuable in the project lead's day-to-day work world.

With a good methodology, the training and coaching requirements are much less than what the certified professionals require. People who find themselves in this multi-role environment should experience a low-incline learning curve. A few days of training, some takeaway tools, and a couple hours of coaching will get them on the road to success.

When it comes to performance expectations for these project leads, you can set them just as high as you would for the certified professionals. This is because the complexity found in medium to large projects is not present in the smaller ones. Go ahead and push them to produce strong results in the three roles as long as you have given them the methodology and training they require.

You've got the right level of attention and support for the certified professionals. Now is the time to bump your level of support for those employees who are performing the same roles, but without a safety net.

Lesson 11

Three Traits of People Who Make Things Happen

There is this notion among companies that everyone should be treated the same. No one should receive preferential treatment or have an advantage. It should be first come, first serve with no short cuts allowed. Processes, rules, and conventions should be followed by everyone at all times.

Some people believe this fully and wait for things to happen for them. Some believe in it partially and like it when they're treated as if they're special, then feel they're victims when they're not. Then there are the few who don't believe in this at all and make things happen. It's not that they like or want to feel special or take advantage of others; they just seek and obtain results when they're needed. Every manager wants a handful of these types of people in their organization. They are the individuals management calls on when they're behind the eight-ball and need someone to pull a rabbit out of the hat.

Let's look at one of those individuals, Linda. One day, Linda's manager came to her with a problem. The person who was responsible for coordinating the week-long new-hire orientation program had just quit and had not done anything to get ready for the orientation that was coming up in two weeks. Preparation for these events usually started eight weeks beforehand. Linda's manager now wanted her to step in and make sure the orientation went off without a hitch.

Linda had coordinated these events in the past, so there was no learning curve, but she needed to secure the speakers, training, social events, and venues. Most preparations fell into place with long hours of hard work. Two items, however, were show stoppers: all training rooms were booked for the three days she needed them, and no tried-and-true keynote speakers were available for the kickoff. Linda went to Rick, the person responsible for scheduling the training rooms, and asked him if he could somehow free up a room for her. The next day, Rick called Linda and told her he cancelled a scheduled class so she could have the room. Then Linda got a call from Marcia, a speaker she contacted a few days earlier. Marcia had decided to cancel her vacation plans and speak on opening night. The new-hire orientation went as well as any other had and Linda got a little bonus for making it happen.

You don't know the full story of Linda yet, so read on to see how the following three traits led to her success.

1) Be Likable

People do things for those they like. It's the number one reason people get preferential treatment. It's also the number one complaint of those who *don't* get preferential treatment. It's the reason the government and corporations instituted formal procurement practices. People were buying from people they liked regardless of the cost. Being liked is not something you're born with. You have to pay attention to how people respond to you and change your behavior when you do things others don't like. What you didn't know about Linda is that she was a very likable person. She was moderately outgoing, played on the department's coed softball team, and went out to lunch Fridays with her peers. She had strong relationships with lots of people.

2) Be Generous

A major consideration people have when they decide to do something for someone else is the "account balance" between the two. The account is a ledger of favors given, offset by favors received. People who are generous have an abundance mentality and are prone to do more for others than what others have done for them. They tend to live life with lots of favors owed. Ungenerous people live life with their account balances at zero (or less) and have little chance of securing any favors. To develop an abundance mentality, you have to shed the belief that people are out to take advantage of you or keep you from getting what is entitled to you. That belief is what makes people stingy and ungenerous. Linda was a generous person. On a number of occasions she had switched to a less than desirable training room so Rick could accommodate another person who needed the better room. He just returned the favor.

3) Be a Master of Leverage

Leverage allows small efforts to generate big results. Masters of leverage see leverage points in all situations. They see the obvious ones on the surface and the ones a couple levels below. There are two types of leverage: those that lead to goodwill by appealing to others through win-win solutions, and those that lead to resentment because of intimidation. Obviously, it's best to use those that lead to goodwill. Gaining favors through leverage is an art that improves with practice. The reason Marcia decided to cancel her vacation and speak was because Linda was on the conference committee of a trade association for which Marcia wanted to speak. Linda told her if she spoke at the new hire orientation kickoff, she would make sure Marcia got a speaking invitation to the trade association conference.

You can't fake these traits. They have to be at the core of who you are. People who fake them tend to be narcissistic and care only about themselves. Their actions come off as disingenuous and slimy. They ultimately never deliver and therefore aren't able to make things happen. Be one of the few in your organization who makes things happen: Genuinely develop these three traits in your life.

Lesson 12

Don't Forget About the Project Environment

Projects are neither good nor bad: they're neutral. They succeed or fail because of what team members do to them; the skills each team member brings to a project affect its ultimate success. Most executives understand this, which is why they spend money on training because raising the skill level of team members increases the odds that projects will succeed more often. But, even a highly skilled project team will struggle if the project environment they work in is not conducive to project work.

What is a project environment? In a nutshell, it's made up of three elements: the **processes, tools,** and **culture** of an organization. The project environment can help or hinder a project team's ability to produce desired results; and, more importantly, it's often not addressed by executives when they try to raise an organization's proficiency at delivering project results.

Let's examine each of these elements in more detail. An organization's **processes** describe how to manage a project, define business requirements, produce deliverables, and test and implement a final product, to name a few. Processes are the means by which an organization obtains consistency and maintains governance over how work gets accomplished. An organization's **tools** assist in carrying out the processes through automation. They bring about efficiency and enhance the skills of team members. Finally, an organization's **culture** is much less tangible, but it has a great deal more influence over any given project team. It drives individual behavior through observed, unwritten laws.

So what happens when companies invest only in training for their employees and don't address their project environments? The project results—when the project is completed—are improved, but executives tend to become disappointed because they were hoping for *more* improvement. Systemation has helped numerous companies with their project environments and all of them have followed the same path—regardless of the advice we gave them. We now believe that even though this path may not be the most efficient way, it may be the only path to obtaining the desired outcome. Let me give you an example:

Steve was our project sponsor who hired us to help him with his organization's project environment. He wanted us to integrate Microsoft Project's Enterprise Server after we had trained nearly half his 500 project managers on general project management skills. We advised Steve to first focus on the project management processes, but he believed he didn't need to because his project managers would use the processes we taught, without customizing them to fit the company's process. After installing the server, it mostly sat idle except for the few who used it in various non-conventional ways.

Steve soon realized he did need to develop his own project management processes, so he put together a committee that developed a full suite of them. The committee did so in detail and even ensured the processes integrated well with Microsoft Project. We advised him that the processes were too restrictive and did not allow for the right level of autonomy needed to function in a project-based organization. We also thought they needed to be more oriented toward results than actions. As expected, the project managers became frustrated with the processes because they were too restrictive and did not have the flexibility to meet a wide variety of situations.

Steve saw that the process reflected a culture that was not consistent with how project work got done at his organization. He ended up spending several months helping his management team change the way it managed its employees. The management team learned to take a more hands-off approach and use project results and gate points to evaluate and take corrective action. They then revised the project management processes to integrate better with the new culture they had established.

Obviously, from this story, you can tell that it would have been quicker for Steve to change his organization's culture first, then create the right type of processes, and then select and integrate the right tools. That old saying of "you don't know what you don't know" applies here. I don't think Steve could have gotten to the end result any other way.

Steve ultimately realized a much greater degree of project success throughout his organization, but he had to put in the effort and time to make it a reality. Relying completely on training will not get the project results you're looking for. You have to address the project environment too.

Lesson 13

Define Your Project into a Box

The hardest thing to do when launching a project is to define it into a box. Yes, I said define it INTO a box. When a project starts, there are lots of interviews with stakeholders. Every one of them has a vision for what the project should include. This gets added, that gets added and pretty soon you have a big hairy monster on your hands, one that needs a serious haircut, not just a little off the top.

Project managers and business analysts are responsible for defining a single vision for the project, a vision with little ambiguity that all parties can realistically accomplish and accept. I'm not talking about detailed requirements here; I'm talking about the description of the project's scope that is created for the project plan at the beginning of the project. It's what points the project in a clear direction and provides boundaries to contain future activities.

Most folks think the key to removing ambiguity in a project's scope is to define the project in minute detail. This is not only hard to do at the start of a project, it also doesn't take advantage of another way to define a project's scope through contrasting. Let me use an analogy to make my point clear.

An HDTV screen's quality is determined by its resolution and contrast. Its resolution is the number of pixels that make up the screen. Everyone today knows that HDTV is better than regular TV because

45

HDTV has twice as many pixels. This gives the picture its detail. Contrast is the second contributor to screen quality and is the difference between how bright a white, illuminated pixel is compared to a blank black pixel. That's why plasma screens are better than LCD screens. This gives the picture its crispness.

To improve the quality of your project scope definitions, you must work on the contrast too. Talk about what is *not* a part of the project in as much detail as you talk about what *is* in a project's scope. Use the exclusions area of the project plan. This may seem like you're being a "naysayer" but, believe me, it will bring out all the points of contention related to your project's scope. You see, people have the tendency to assume you meant to include what they wanted in your scope definition, even if you don't specifically include it. If you specifically state that the project is not going to include some aspect of scope and someone disagrees with you, you're now able to resolve the issue and create one vision.

The more you describe what is not in a project's scope, the less ambiguity you'll have and the closer you'll be to putting your project into a well-defined box.

Lesson 14

Know a Person's Power Base

You have probably heard of Myers-Briggs, Social Style, DISC, and other personality-style assessments. They're great for helping us realize that people are different, and that by paying attention to others' styles, you can work more effectively with them. Many people have benefited from these personality categorization systems, but there's another factor that sits on top of these styles and drives them to some degree. It's a person's **power base**.

When we were very young, our parents were our protectors and builders of our self-esteem. As we got older, we interacted with others more on our own and started to develop a foundation for operating in social settings. It was a lifeline that helped us get through our middle school and high school years. By early adulthood, we had fully established our own base of power that would aid us in social settings by attracting the admiration of others and limiting the potential for harm.

As we move deeper into adulthood, our power base becomes so integrated into our very core that we no longer realize we have one. When our power base is stroked, we feel very good, and when it's attacked we become defensive. In fact, we have to be careful not to step on a person's power base because they tend to overreact disproportionately to the threat. But the great thing is you don't even need an assessment to identify a person's power base; you just need to observe him or her.

Why is it so important to know a person's power base? Because it can be very useful in building support from someone and keeping us out of harm's way by inadvertently crossing it. However, keep in mind that one should never use this information to manipulate others, only to enrich interaction with them.

Below, I describe six prominent power bases. There are others, such as humor and athleticism, but these six cover the majority of people. Each type includes a short description of what a person's standard behavior is, what they do when confronted, and who they appeal to in social settings.

1) Aggression

People who are intimidators like confrontation and deal with it directly. They're not afraid to say things that other people might shy away from. They will get in your face and force you to engage them. When confronted, they will attack harder. There's no backing down. They attract other people who have the same type of power base and people who want additional protection.

2) Intelligence

Intellects are typically smarter and know more than most people. They like talking about difficult subjects and are lifetime learners. They will challenge others when they witness errors or misinformation. If someone else starts the discussion on a topic, they will ultimately end up leading it. When their intellect is challenged they will bombard the aggressor with tons of information and facts in an attempt to undermine their credibility. They attract anyone who values learning and has an interest in a variety of subjects.

3) Niceness

Lots of people are nice. But these folks know *only* how to be nice. They literally cannot show outward anger toward anybody. As a result, they don't experience many threats, but when they do, they tend to display victim behavior. They drum up support from those around them and get others to own and express their internal anger. People in this category get along with everyone and, as a result, attract others of all kinds.

4) Physical Beauty

A person is born with physical beauty, but these people take it to a new level. They work hard at keeping themselves at a specific level of attraction. If they find themselves in a tough spot, they kick into another gear and turn on the charm to get themselves out of it. They know how to leverage their beauty to get the most attention and support from others. Regardless of their personality or character flaws, they always know there's a subset of people who will ignore those flaws just to be close to their beauty.

5) Hiding

People who rely on hiding are usually introverts too. They don't tend to engage others often, don't express their opinions, and generally keep to themselves. They would rather be on the sidelines observing things around them. If they're confronted, they quickly acquiesce and try to hide even more. They strive to attract no one and establish friendships only with others in this category and only after a long period of time.

6) Producing

People in this category are doers. They work hard and produce a lot. You may think this is just a good work ethic, but these folks are compelled to produce. If you challenge them, they will draw upon their last several months of deliverables and quote to you how many hours they have put in. They tend to associate with other producers and look down on people who are sub-standard producers.

As with all behavior-driven systems, there are individuals who don't display the exact behaviors described in these categories. Some display behaviors from two or more different types, and others don't display any of the behaviors. For the majority, however, there are usually observable behaviors that can help you navigate your social settings by simply keeping the different power base categories in mind and applying them to the people around you.

What types of power bases do you experience each day at work? What different methods do you use to communicate with these different categories of people? What power base category do you fall into?

Lesson 15

Employment's Funny Little Dynamics

E mployment: a simple contract between an employer and an employee. The employee agrees to perform some set of activities and, in return, the employer agrees to compensate them for their performance. Sounds pretty simple, right? That's because we haven't considered the dynamics generated by job security, an employee's desires, and the loyalty the employer seeks. What it really comes down to is that neither party wants to be caught off guard by the other if the contract is abolished. It's fine if it ends on their terms, but they definitely do not want to be surprised.

When it's played out daily in the work environment, employers believe that because they give employees a job, they should be loyal and not leave. If an employee tries to leave or actually does so, employers judge them as ungrateful and uncommitted. On the other hand, employees believe that because they trust their employers, they should not have to worry about job security. If for some reason they are "let go," they think that trust has been violated.

In either case, the biggest problem with these situations is not with the employee who is willingly leaving or let go, it's the relationship of the employer with the employees who remain. These relationships often get stressed, resulting in "us vs. them," manager vs. worker friction.

What we have here at the core is a clear case of unhealthy expectations. One party is seeking safety by attempting to remove choice from the other. Instead of taking responsibility and putting in the effort to influence the other party's choice, they attempt to shame the other into one choice, the one that favors them. Let's look at this from each party's side.

Employers

Employers want the benefit that comes from loyalty. This is understandable. They prefer to not spend the time, effort, and money it takes to go through the hiring process. They don't like the disruption that occurs in their organizations when someone departs and leaves a hole in their operations. They like to know that the training investment they make will provide a good return.

If employers want the benefits that come from employee loyalty, they need to do what it takes to obtain it—and it's the employee who gets to decide what it takes. It means employers need to give generously beyond what is already established in the employment contract. Just because they gave someone a job, it does not result in loyalty. It takes caring for them individually, knowing about their families, building a strong sense of community at work, and not always responding to things based on corporate policy when a unique or critical situation arises.

When someone does leave the organization, celebrate it with them. Be the lead in throwing the going-away party. Keep in touch with them after they leave to see how they're doing. This will speak volumes to the employees who are still with you.

Employees

Employees want to have a secure feeling related to their employment. This, too, is understandable. Their employment fulfills many of the items they need for their and their families' existence. The person who has the most influence in this situation is the employee. They are the ones who are responsible for and in control of their performance. It has nothing to do with trusting their employers, since trust is about someone acting consistently with what they promise or expound. Employees can expect and trust their employers to give them the compensation they agreed on, allow them to take time off that was previously approved, treat them with respect, and many other things. They cannot trust an employer to continue their employment if their performance is subpar; it's the employer who gets to decide this.

Performance is more than just how well you perform the tasks and responsibilities you're assigned. It also has to do with how flexible your work schedule is when you have to get a critical project completed, how much effort you put into broadening your knowledge and skills, how good a team player you are, and how well you get along with others in the organization. These are all within your sphere of control.

There's a great chance you're going to be an employee or an employer for some time. You might as well make it easier on yourself and those you work with by mastering the dynamics that surround employment. Instead of having unhealthy expectations, take responsibility for yourself and earn your security through your good actions.

Lesson 16

A Project Manager's ROI

A ll project managers see their jobs differently. Some are very lofty in describing their role; others seem lost, still trying to discover it. There is talk of making customers happy, working with users, managing risk, and many other activities. But, if you ask directors of project managers: "What is the role of a project manager?", they are very clear: Plan the project, put a stick in the ground, and meet expectations.

A formal definition of project management is "predicting, with as much certainty as is possible or required, the project's scope, time, and cost at completion, and then embracing reality and influencing activities to meet these predictions."

It's a very scary thing for project managers to predict where a project will end up because it holds them accountable. But predicting is imperative. If there isn't an end point for the project manager to drive toward, there won't be any management or direction of the project, only drifting. Who wants a project drifter leading their project?

There's no such thing as "one size fits all" when it comes to project management. Every project has different constraints, requiring different levels of certainty when it comes to predicting and meeting scope, time, and cost. This is important because the amount of effort expended in managing a project is directly related to the amount of certainty obtained. The relationship between certainty and effort is known as **Project Management ROI**. With just a little effort, you can achieve a fair amount of certainty. The more effort you apply, the more certainty you obtain. Today's project managers often identify how much time they have available to manage a project and let the certainty be determined as a result. This tends to lead to poor project results and dissatisfaction across the board. In fact, for this approach, the average cost overrun is 189%; time overrun 222%; and scope reduction, 61%. While these results may be reasonable for some low-priority projects, higher-priority projects require more certainty.

The proper way to approach a project is to first identify the level of certainty required, then let the amount of effort be determined as a result. This approach will drive the person who is selected to manage the project, the expectations that are set for them, and whether they manage it full time or part time. It also drives the amount of process and rigor the project manager follows.

Know the importance of your project, determine the certainty needed, get the right project manager, have them predict the end result, and expend the required effort to bring it to a reality. That's the pathway to project success.

Lesson 17

Holding People Accountable

You've heard the talk in the hallways. "He's not holding so and so accountable." "They never deliver on time." "If I were the project manager I'd sure hold them accountable."

Or, "If they worked directly for me I could hold them accountable." "That's the problem with this company. No one works directly for their supervisors." "There always seems to be an easy fix, yet no one seems to make it work."

It's sad, but true. Project managers are at the mercy of others when it comes to producing a finished product on time and within budget because they don't produce the product themselves. Project managers actually coordinate and integrate the work of others into something bigger: the end product. Getting team members and suppliers to be accountable for their pieces of the project puzzle is paramount for project success, but this is easier said than done. So, what usually happens is project team members are late, over budget, and deliver less than what's required. This, in turn, causes the project to be late and over budget, and leads to an end product that's less than what the client wants. As a result, project managers are not being accountable for their project results, causing them to catch heat from their management. The process of establishing and holding people accountable can be a source of tension, frustration, pointed words, and angst. As tough as it may be, there are steps companies can take with project team members, suppliers, and management to maximize the opportunity for success.

The definition of accountability is *being responsible to someone or for some activity*. It's commitment — an agreement between two parties, one providing something to the other that's either tangible or conceptual. To build a healthy agreement, you must set clear expectations, provide complete and accurate information, and remain open to negotiation. If any of these components doesn't exist in an initial agreement between two parties, the opportunity for success is greatly diminished.

Let's examine the elements of good accountability practices through a personal example, painting your house:

You're not a professional painter, so you hire someone, Pete the painter. Pete shows up at the agreed-upon time – so far so good. You relay the house's history of paint jobs, and express what you envision for this job regarding colors, detail, prep work, and timeframe for completion. You relay project particulars, such as the neighbors having forbidden the placement of ladders on their grass when painting the sides of the house. Also, you don't want him painting when your guests are in town visiting you for two days next month.

Pete then explains his expertise and how he can meet your needs. He sounds like the kind of worker you'd like to hire, so he gives you his initial bid. It's more than you budgeted for, so you ask him if he can lower the cost. But for a lower price, he says he can only paint the house's body, and you'll have to paint the trim. You need to save money where you can, so you agree to these terms and the lowered price, and hope he follows through as promised. Before he leaves, you tell Pete you'll monitor the work daily.

In establishing this agreement, you've set the foundation for holding Pete accountable. You have:

1. **Provided complete and accurate information** by giving him the house's history and your neighbors' restrictions. This is crucial because when either party withholds or provides misleading information, the planned course of action becomes invalid and commitments cannot be met.
2. **Set clear expectations** by outlining items such as the related costs, timeframe, and project direction. Expectations are pivotal to accountability and are usually expressed in terms of time or deadlines, cost, and scope (what the final product should look like). Pete must finish the job in two weeks and for $4,000.
3. **Remained open to negotiation.** It's only after you've provided accurate, complete information and stated your expectations that Pete will be able to offer an estimate. At that point, he must be allowed to negotiate so that when the agreement is set, he takes ownership in his choices and final decisions. Without negotiation, it would be absurd of you to demand that Pete paint your house to a certain level of quality, within a specific period of time, and for a price tag of your choosing.

As in this personal example, when you're a project manager you'll want to ensure success by setting guidelines, then reinforcing them with these three additional steps:

1. **Provide team members with an understanding of the project's envisioned "big picture"** by clearly communicating their roles in making that big picture a reality. When employees realize how their efforts, no matter how small, contribute to the big picture, they'll respect and take ownership of their work, and feel motivated to see it succeed.

2. **Keep an eye on assignments and progress** by obtaining periodic status reports based on a level of reasonable trust. For example, if a project manager knows a team member is reliable, he will take a hands-off approach to track the team member's progress. However, you might need to "babysit" less competent team members who are given the same assignment. If too much trust is shown when it isn't warranted, team members may slack off. If too little trust is shown when it isn't warranted, they'll feel you're nagging for no reason. Both situations lead to decreased employee morale, possibly resulting in a distrust of your integrity, which will ultimately undermine the good intentions of the established healthy agreement.

3. **Infuse staff with the desire to commit to the assigned job or activity** by offering valuable incentives, such as a box of donuts, coveted tickets to a show or sporting event, or a gift certificate to a favorite restaurant. To enhance bonds with the project manager, sometimes appreciation can be shown to teams in advance of an upcoming request. They'll connect better with the project manager and feel obligated to perform at maximum capacity when the opportunity presents itself.

Even if you follow all these practices, you may still find team members failing to deliver as promised. Don't be surprised. Most of the time, team members intend to deliver or act upon a healthy project agreement, but poor professional skills or uncontrollable environmental issues derail the outcome, and accountability falters.

If you're finding that accountability is still lacking, be careful not to assume that team members don't care when they don't deliver since most of them genuinely care and feel committed to both the project manager and the project. Instead, consider these top five reasons for missed accountability:

1. **Underdeveloped time management skills**. An employee might lose focus, dawdle, or forget various tasks.

2. **Inadequate job estimation skills**. An overly optimistic team member may agree to complete a particular task without truly understanding its scope, thus underestimating the amount of time it will take to complete the task.

3. **Lack of project domain expertise**. For instance, an expert in a certain discipline may be able to complete a specific task in one week, whereas a novice may require two weeks because of countless reworks.

4. **Failure to understand a task or activity's priority in relationship to other work**. This typically occurs when individuals can't grasp the impact of their current duties and how it relates to the "big picture." They view this project element as unimportant when it's actually crucial to success.

5. **Poor attitude**. It's rare, but sometimes employees simply don't care, put forth effort or feel a sense of "project passion." For instance, one worker might simply dislike the project manager. This is most commonly manifested in passive-aggressive behaviors, such as "putting on a face of cooperation and concern," then undermining the project manager's efforts in discreet and subtle ways.

Perhaps one of the least enjoyable aspects of the project manager's job regarding failed accountability is analyzing the mishap's implications and determining its root cause. The breakdown could simply be a fluke; or something or someone, including you, might truly be responsible. But remember, your mission is not to determine fault for the sole purpose of assigning blame.

Consider the 1986 tragedy of the space shuttle Challenger. NASA collected data and immediately set to solve the reason why the explosion occurred, dismissing the media's probe for who was to blame. That's not saying individuals weren't responsible for the disaster. However, if the engineers and scientists had sat around dwelling upon blame, they may never have been able to uncover what happened and how to avoid future tragedies.

Once you have identified the root cause in a situation of failed accountability, you must establish another project agreement of what is expected. In addition to that agreement, what was originally promised is still required for your project's success. But this time, you must check up more frequently on the project's status to adequately monitor this second agreement.

Sometimes, despite numerous attempts to uphold accountability, a trend of missed commitments develops with individuals. While these situations may seem hopeless, remember that it's your job to boost the team's commitment level to achieve project results. Options include:

- **Motivation.** The least aggressive approach to boosting employee commitment, this approach is reasonably effective but requires extra effort on your part. Coach each individual on their skill deficits and help them deliver on their commitments. Or consider offering additional enticements to increase the team members' desire to deliver as agreed. Either of these approaches will enhance the relationship between you and team members.

- **Coercion**. Capable of producing immediate, noticeable results, this tactic can strain the relationship between you and your team member. For example, if you're unhappy with a team member's work, you might give him or her a poor performance review. A project manager can also coerce change by complaining to the team member's boss if that person doesn't work directly for the project manager. Another great approach is publicly discussing the situation, revealing the cause for the failed accountability without using a tone of blame. This tactic puts peer pressure on the team member to take ownership of the situation and change it.

If motivation and coercion fail, and the negative trend continues to plague the project's success, look for a different environment in which that troublesome employee may work, or inflict the least amount of damage to the team's productivity. The key is to reduce the impact or totally eliminate the source of accountability failure. Some project managers might think it's OK to intimidate someone into job commitment (such as physical threats or extreme verbal confrontations), but keep in mind that it's illegal to do so. If you're even tempted to follow such a path, remember that a better option is to seek the employee's termination or an in-house transfer.

As the project manager, you must master the art of accountability. Despite challenges, you do have the ability to deliver on your executives' expectations. When you're feeling trapped, hopeless, and uninspired by your responsibilities as project manager, don't give in. Instead, take the appropriate steps to successfully hold people accountable – it's one of the things that turn good project managers into great ones.

Lesson 18

Your Biggest Project Risk is Poor Project Management

One of Systemation's most highly sought after, single-discipline classes within project management is risk management. Directors are hot on it; they feel their PMs are weak in risk management because of a common pattern they witness: Projects are not being completed as expected and the main culprit, it seems, is unexpected events, or unforeseen risks that plague these projects. Directors believe that if PMs receive training in risk management, they will be more able to foresee these events and avoid them.

What directors do not fully know is that these unforeseen events are not due to poor risk management skills but **poor fundamental project management skills**. This is what happens behind the scenes on a mismanaged project: The project manager gets surprised when he becomes aware that his project's schedule or quality of the deliverable is missing the mark. In an effort to draw attention away from himself, the PM creates a story based on events that could not have been seen and mitigated. These stories are not total fiction; they often contain a good portion of fact but are told in a manner that supports the project manager's position that he was the victim of these unforeseen events.

What probably happened is that the PM did not have a handle on the details of the project's current state. He also did not pay attention to the future work that might be impacted by the current reality. As a result, the current reality was vague and its impact on the future was even more so. In this situation, everything becomes a surprise.

Symptoms of poor project management display themselves in several specific ways. Here are a few:

- Not breaking down the deliverables into a detailed set of tasks;
- Not identifying the dependencies between tasks;
- Not knowing what tasks have been completed;
- Not knowing how much more remains to be completed on incomplete tasks;
- Not curtailing scope expansion based on the project's scope statement;
- Not adjusting future estimates based on estimating error trends;
- Not adjusting future work based on current reality and its impact on project completion;
- Not tracking external dependencies; and
- Not knowing if the promised availability of partial resources is being met.

If we apply the risk management process to these risks, it would go like this: Risk identification tells us poor project management is a potential risk, risk assessment tells us the potential impact is extremely high, and the risk mitigation plan is to ensure PMs practice good project management fundamentals.

This is easier said than done, but still very doable. Five actions must be implemented to ensure PMs practice good project management fundamentals:

1. **Project managers must receive training in the fundamentals.** The training must cover project planning, execution and control, and it must be sufficiently thorough to give them practical understanding of the concepts.

2. **There must be a standard methodology project managers can follow.** It must be appropriately balanced between planning, execution, and control, and be detailed enough to give them a routine to follow that will help overcome the practices of poor project management defined above.

3. **Project managers must have access to software tools that enable them to easily follow the training and methodology provided.**

4. **Project managers must deliver management reports on a routine basis** that are metric-driven and allow management to verify that good project management practices are being followed. Project managers must also provide management with accurate status reports on their projects.

5. **Management must support the practice of project management.** This is much more involved than you think. It means acquiring a working knowledge of project management fundamentals so you can talk the PM's language. It also mean giving PMs the time to do their jobs right and not asking them to take shortcuts or disregard portions of the project management methodology they're following.

In more than 12 years of coaching PMs on live projects every other week for six-month sessions, Systemation has very rarely encountered unforeseen project risks that result in project failure. The reason is that these five actions were instituted within the PMs' organizations and were sustained long after the sessions ended.

The next time a PM plays the victim and blames unforeseen risks, audit him. You'll learn that, most likely, it isn't unforeseen risk that hurt his project; it's poor project management.

Lesson 19

The Elusive High-Performance Team

I n the 1980s, high-performance teams were the craze. Project management was just coming into its own and teams were getting more and more attention, But today, we talk about and observe them with little fanfare. Although high-performance teams have become "untrendy," their importance to projects is still extremely significant.

The continuum of team performance is very broad. Most of us don't really know what a high-performance team looks like because the average employee has never been involved in one (since they're so rare). However, most employees can spot a low-performance team in a heartbeat.

Why is it so rare to witness or experience a high-performance team? Well, many factors have arisen in organizations that inhibit their existence: virtual employees who allow for little face-to-face interaction, matrix environments that encourage allegiance to home organizations instead of project teams, and resource management philosophies and tools that strive for partial assignments and attention. Plus, the price of creating a high-performance team is immense. It takes tremendous amounts of resources and time.

But, with the correct environment and resources, the benefits of high-performance teams are invaluable due to their ability to generate contributions that are greater than the sum of their individual team members. It's all about synergy. Synergy motivates team members through mutual support, generates better solutions through diversity of skills, and sustains performance through shared efforts. Two great examples of successful high-performance teams are revealed in the movie *Miracle on Ice* that details the journey of the 1980 U.S. Olympic hockey team to a gold medal, and in the more recent book *Lone Survivor*, which describes the training and events of a specific Navy SEAL team.

Many factors contribute to teams that reach the high-performance level. The biggest contributors are: a single, well-understood vision; appropriate levels of autonomy; acceptance of diversity in skills, personality, character, and work styles; strong individual performance;s and a mindset that puts the team's interest above those of individual members.

So, in today's environment, what can you hope for from your teams? It depends on your organization and your team's practices. If there are no inhibitors in your organization, and you're practicing traits that encourage high performance, then you can expect some good results. But, if your organization and practices are inhibited, then the best you can hope for is that some work will get accomplished with little negative impact.

This is a clear case of the solutions causing unintended consequences even though they're intended to create benefits in other areas. All of these efforts to optimize resource utilization are undermining the performance of teams and individuals. What is actually meant to create efficiencies is causing inefficiencies. This isn't being done intentionally; it's just a human system error that has to be played out. Unfortunately, you may be stuck in the middle and can't do anything about it. All you *can* do is work to the best of your ability with the team and environment you have.

Hang in there.

Lesson 20

End Users Have Horizon Lines Too

W e have been unfair to end users for far too long. We ask them what they want the application to do for them and they tell us as best they can. Then we get mad at them because they change their minds or bring up additional items later in the project. We've been complaining about this for decades.

I find this situation very similar to one we have experienced in project management. In project management, we've learned from project planning that when you begin a project, the earlier portions of a project's work breakdown structure will always be in greater detail than later portions. That's because we came to realize that projects have **horizon lines**: points in time when more information becomes available, giving us a new context to plan the next section of the project in more detail. In the classic waterfall methodology, these horizon lines tend to line up with the starting points of each phase. The only reason we came to this conclusion is because project managers banged their heads against the wall trying to plan the whole project in detail as if they could see clearly into the future. Repeated failures and frustrations led to the understanding of horizon lines.

Do you think it's time we realize that end users have horizon lines too? In the beginning of a project, the end users are able to visualize the final product, but only in bigger chunks and with little knowledge of the peculiarities that exist several layers down in the details. It's not until the product starts to take shape when they can interact with it and begin to see the subtle implications of decisions they made earlier. We may label this as scope creep, but it's really just them dealing with their own set of horizon lines and starting to change and add requirements. Let's look at an example:

> *Kelly was the business unit's lead representative on a project initiated to create a new customer service application. It was the first time she was in this role. Lucky for her, she was paired with a very seasoned business analyst, Carol. Because of her experience, Carol worked with the project manager to create several demos early in the development phase and add time for some rework. She knew this would allow Kelly to see her initial requirements become enough of a reality to cause her to think through other requirements that the final product would need to be successful. In the end, the final product was a hit and the project manager was able to deliver it within the time frame he planned initially.*

Now, I want to make sure you understand my point here. I'm not making excuses for an end user's lack of hard work. But I *am* pleading for a little grace for their lack of perfection in visualizing the future. Change happens. It's time we plan for it.

Lesson 21

Four Personas Leaders Must Balance to Be Effective

It's no secret that leaders receive a lot of attention. They are involved in highly visible activities, make decisions that affect whole organizations, and interact with countless people. Everything they do is observed by others and, accordingly, contributes to how people perceive them. These perceptions are very important and powerful because they influence others around them.

How employees think a leader will respond to a specific situation influences what they do regarding that situation. Employees ask themselves what the leader's response will be if they deliver late on that project, don't call the client back this week, try something that has not been tried before, take a shortcut on production and deliver a sub-standard product, show up to a meeting late, share bad news, ignore what they were told to do, make a mistake, and many other situation-induced choices. What employees do is not a given and affects an organization's performance, credibility, and reputation.

It's in a leader's best interest to manage these perceptions and use them to get the best and most out of their staff. However, not all perceptions are created equal, and they carry the same level of impact. Knowing the most influential perceptions of employees is the first step in developing and tuning your personas. Highly effective leaders have four equally emphasized personas they promote to their staffs.

They're gracious, demanding, approachable, and revered. Let's look at these personas in detail and how they can impact you.

1) Gracious

This persona is reasonable, patient, forgiving, and caring. It informs others that they try to do good, but at times make mistakes. It knows learning is a process and takes time. It also knows that life is a complex mix of business and personal issues that, at times, trump one another. Others respond to graciousness by trying new things to get better results, giving extra effort when the situation warrants it, and cutting you some slack when you screw up.

2) Demanding

This persona is insistent, rigorous, challenging, and straightforward. It informs people that you know what you want and expect to get it just like that. It pushes people past their perceived limits and shows them they can do more. It also provides direct, unfiltered feedback and consequences that make sure the feedback is remembered. Others respond to the demanding persona by being more intense and purposeful when producing deliverables, prompt with milestones and meetings, and being crisper overall in their performance.

3) Approachable

This persona is transparent, humble, restrained, and attentive. It informs people that you want them to know who you are and you want to know them too. It encourages people to come to you and share their thoughts, ideas, and observations. It also lets others know you won't blow things out of proportion and overreact. Others respond to approachability by being more likely to let down their guard when they're around you, allowing you to see more of what holds them back professionally, being more forthright and truthful with information, and enjoying your company.

4) Revered

This persona is commanding, powerful, courageous, and capable. It reminds people that you're the leader and those who follow you will benefit from this. It tells people they have a strong advocate and can rely on you to remove barriers when needed. It also makes them feel a part of something bigger than themselves and their roles. Others will respond to reverence by often buying into your vision more, looking out for your best interests and therefore the organization's best interests, and being proud of where they work.

Each of these personas offsets the influence of one or more of the other personas. This is a good thing as any one of the personas in full force is not a good influence on employees and affects them negatively. Having all four in balance can yield the best possible impact on the staff. Most leaders are strong in two or three of these personas and weak in the rest. As a result, the personas are not balanced and are not optimally influencing others.

The good thing is that personas can be learned with discipline, effort, feedback, and changes in behavior. But don't think you can fake these personas. Fake personas are not reliable and will produce perceptions that are not congruent with the true personas, resulting in employees being influenced negatively. It's better to put in the work to produce the results you desire. Now that you know what the target is, take a shot at getting there.

Lesson 22

Become a Value-Driven Organization

W ork has sure changed over the years. Technology has given us more access to information and faster ways to analyze, design, and develop that information. It has also blurred the lines between personal and work time. Our work environment has become much more casual too, from dress to business protocol.

However, one thing that has not changed much is how we perceive work. Work is still viewed very generically. A minimum amount of time has to be put in during a defined time period. This is when the company owns its employees and expects a reasonable amount of effort be expended. Each person is given a specific number of days off, a set of health benefits, and policies to follow. In the end, a person puts in a fair day's work and gets a fair day's pay. For the most part, everyone is treated the same with the exception of a few perks based on longevity with the company.

Within a specific skill set, there is believed to be little variability in work since there is little deviation in effort and hours. If the only thing that separates one person from another is their salary, then work is a commodity where:

$$\text{work} = \frac{\text{amount of effort expended}}{\text{number of hours put in}}$$

There are two problems with this view. First, with commodities, margins must be tightly managed so costs (salaries) are always under pressure to be lowered while maintaining existing production levels (work). Often, this environment leads to an unintended downward spiral in production and quality. The second and more important problem is that work is seen as the product. But customers don't buy work, they buy *value*. Shouldn't our view of work be aligned with what we're trying to create for our customers?

However, if we focus on the value we're trying to create for our customers, it forces us to understand the value chain within our organization and each person's link in that chain. With this perception of work, value becomes the desired end for each person in which:

$$\text{value} = \frac{\text{benefit provided}}{\text{cost of producing}}$$

Having employees focused on the value they generate makes them responsible for ensuring the benefit they produce hits the mark and is much greater than the cost (salary) expended. Plus, it drives employees to focus their effort on activities that will apply greater value to the organization's value chain, hence increasing the value to the customer.

This switch to a value-driven organization does not come easy, and changes will need to be made. Specifically, you should:

- **Dethrone effort in your workplace.** The current view of work focuses on effort, which is a means to an end. Value-driven organizations focus on results, yielding benefits. Play down each employee's number of hours worked, work schedule, and number of years with the company. Get comfortable with the idea that someone could create the same value in two hours that another can create a week, and that it's OK. You have to start treating people differently, seeking ways to help each person create the most value possible.

- **Highlight each employee's link in the value chain.** Each employee should know and understand their link at its purest level. An employee's primary focus should be on consistently providing value to the chain. If they're sick, want to go on vacation, or attend some training, it's their responsibility for ensuring that consistency.

- **View an employee's life as a blend of personal time and work.** You expect work time to interrupt personal time when there is a great need. You should also expect an employee's personal life to interrupt work. You can no longer have the view that you own that employee during business hours. If they're surfing the web for clothes or leaving to watch their child's activities during business hours, you should have no problem with it.

- **Make employees responsible for their own growth.** It's the employees' responsibility to prepare themselves for generating higher levels of benefit. The organization may provide the funds for certain training, but the employee needs to identify what they want to learn and how they'll learn it.

- **Know your employees' value.** You and each employee need to be keenly aware of the benefits they have provided and are providing today. You must also be aware of their past and current salary levels. When the gap between those two begins to diminish (assuming benefit is higher than salary), then the value they're producing is diminishing too. Something has to change or they won't be around, regardless of their longevity with the company. If they're underpaid, this needs to be corrected as well.

Many highly respected and successful organizations have begun the transition of becoming value-driven. And, it's highly likely this transition can be accomplished without interfering with your overall company policies. Go ahead and jump in! It will be a rich and rewarding experience for you and your employees.

Lesson 23

Estimating: Why We'll Never Get it Right

E stimating ... predicting ... forecasting. These are three different words with three things in common:

1. They establish a position on the future with some margin of error;
2. All are used for planning purposes, and aim to help companies prepare for the future; and
3. We know their accuracy and successes are broad and varying.

The reason we use and rely on these techniques is that they help us to be more efficient and produce greater profits. This is one of the top priorities of current business. If we know how long it will take to develop something, we'll know when to shift resources to something new. If we know how much additional revenue we'll make next year, we can determine what budgets can be allocated to jump ahead of our competition. If we know what product functionality a customer wants, we can build just that and avoid developing unwanted capabilities.

Nowhere is this truer than with project management, which relies heavily on estimating: what tasks need to be accomplished, how long each task will take, how many resources need to be on the project to complete it on time, what will be built, and what the best approach is to building the product. Project success often relies on our ability to estimate.

We all realize that perfect estimating accuracy is unrealistic. What we don't realize is just how wrong our expectations on estimating accuracy truly are. As a result, we search and search for better ways of estimating, hoping we'll find the one method that will make us significantly better estimators. But this will never happen, so perhaps we should focus on adjusting our expectations.

Unfortunately, we have a habit of departing from rational thinking and acting in ways that prevent us from accommodating a reality that allows us to feel we're doing a good job at estimating. Here are four ways we depart from rational thinking:

1. **There is much more randomness in projects than we want to believe.** Nassim Nicholas Taleb wrote two fantastic books that establish this truth: *Fooled by Randomness* and *The Black Swan*. As a result of randomness, our estimating accuracy, at best, will follow the bell curve, with a good portion of estimates a standard deviation from perfect and with some falling at the outer edges of the curve. At worst, our estimating error can be a black swan event, something that comes in tens of times greater than our estimate. Either way, our projects zig and zag all over the place because of the flow of randomness. Funny thing, Teleb says the best way to protect yourself from randomness is to build slack into your system. In reality, there isn't much chance of that happening since slack is the very inefficiency we don't want.

2. **We don't invest in getting better at estimating.** It's amazing how little project data we keep and analyze. All we need are time and a few processes to make it happen, and if we did this we would have a better idea of the standard deviations in estimating errors on tasks, phases, and project completions.

We would also become better estimators of scope, time, and cost on common projects, for sure. If we implemented sophisticated predictive models, such as the Monte Carlo method, we would know what the outer edges of our estimating errors could be on complex projects. For some reason, these approaches are not valued enough in organizations, but it never stops us from passing judgment on people's performance based on incomplete or bad data.

3. **Our expectations are inversely proportional to project scale.** Projects with longer durations and greater complexity have more aggressive expectations than shorter-duration, less complex projects. For instance, say we ask Jack to estimate how long it will take for a baseball dropped from the top of the Empire State building to hit the ground. He estimates 20 seconds and, upon doing so, it takes just 9.8 seconds. Most would think the estimate was fairly close. He was only off a few seconds. Now let's ask Jill to estimate how long it would take for her and a baseball to sail from a peer on Hawaii's main island to Los Angeles, fly to New York City, and go to the top of the Empire State building before she drops the baseball. She estimates 17 days; it actually takes 10.4 days. Most would say she estimated poorly since she is off by almost 7 days. The reality is: Jill was off by only 38% while Jack was off by 51%. These misconceptions of relativity don't make sense, but it's how we think. This reality becomes especially painful when you consider projects that have the most impact on our businesses are more complex and longer in duration, making them harder to estimate, and requiring smaller margins of error to be successful.

4. **We put too much emphasis on human will and competence.** At its roots, estimating error contains human will and competence, but it also contains randomness. It's true that human will can heal a person faster or help them overcome major

life catastrophes. It's also true that highly skilled individuals can outperform their lesser peers two to one. However, randomness plays a much bigger role in estimating error than we think. We have all heard of teams coming together to overcome extreme obstacles, but what we don't know is if randomness actually aligned in favor of their success and thus played a bigger role. I wonder if we put so much emphasis on human will and competence because we're so afraid that if we don't, people will slack off and not perform as well.

It may seem like a pessimistic or fatalistic view, but there's a good chance we will never embrace reality and become comfortable with the estimating accuracy that exists in a random world. It would mean we'd have to minimize human will and effort, rely on data-driven criteria for estimating error that focus on percentages, and assign estimating handicaps to projects with longer durations and more complexity. It's a daunting challenge and that's why we'll never get it right.

Anyone up for the challenge?

Lesson 24

The Power of the Question

I t's precious to watch a young child learn. They ask questions that reveal their naivete and inquisitiveness. Question after question, their minds churn taking in information and formulating new questions. There's a lot of power in the questions children ask, and because of this they are rewarded with information for growth.

As adults, the power of questions resides more in answering them, specifically questions that reveal information hidden within us. Self-discovery is always a more powerful agent for growth than receiving information from outside sources. But self-discovery requires a catalyst, a person insightful enough to ask a discovery question instead of giving direct answers or feedback. It requires more effort to ask a discovery question, but it also offers more benefits to the person requesting the feedback. Let's look at two of the most common situations where discovery questions are most valuable: when we have judgments about others and when we're asked for direct feedback.

Judging Others

We all make judgments about people we encounter in life: he was rude to the sales person, she likes the limelight too much, etc. For those we're close to, both professionally and personally, our judgments carry more weight. Giving straight feedback to a coworker, subordinate, or friend may be efficient, but it can be received with defensiveness and resentment. Neither of these emotions will allow the person to learn and grow. For them, self-discovery is a much more acceptable means for realizing faults. When you want to address a judgment you have regarding another person, it may be more beneficial to ask a discovery question that helps the person see how their actions or words will affect others, rather than give direct feedback. There are definitive times when direct feedback is the best approach, but discovery questions can be very powerful in many circumstances.

For example, Jennifer was talking with her friend, Lisa, about how little respect her boss has for her personal time. He calls her nights and weekends, asking her questions about work. Sometimes Jennifer has school events for her daughter that she wants to attend after work and her boss will ask her to complete a large project just before she's about to leave for the day. Jennifer continued describing her plight by telling Lisa how frustrated and hurt she is with her boss, but is somehow reluctant to tell him how she feels. Lisa remembered back to when Jennifer accepted the job, excited that it included a large potential bonus every year. It was clear to Lisa that Jennifer likes the money aspect of the job, but resents the level of work it requires. Instead of telling Jennifer this directly, and further angering her, Lisa chose to ask Jennifer a discovery question: "Jennifer, if you did not have the big potential bonus coming next month, how would you respond to your boss's time requests?" Jennifer thought for a moment and said she would tell him he was being disrespectful of her time and would set stronger boundaries on when she would work. Thinking more, she then told Lisa that it appears her boss is not the issue. The issue actually had to do with her needing to decide if the money is worth the amount of time she has to work to earn it. Lisa sat back and marveled at how quickly Jennifer resolved this issue for herself.

Direct Feedback

People often ask for our feedback on something they're working on. It may be a problem they're trying to solve or a plan they've put together. It could even be reviewing any old deliverable they're responsible for. What they are looking for is specifics that would improve what they're working on. When offering feedback you could do just that: Give them straight feedback. But a more powerful option would be to ask a discovery question. In this situation, a question, will force them to consider how they approached their work, resulting in growth and reducing the need for future feedback. Here again, self-discovery is always more enlightening than a straight answer.

For example, Jerry was interrupted by one of his employees, Mark, who asked for some of Jerry's time to talk through a product evaluation he was working on. Mark began by telling Jerry about the two products' capabilities. He continued by communicating how hard it has been for him to choose the better product between the two. Jerry soon realized that Mark was focusing too much on the products' capabilities and not enough on how the products would positively or negatively impact the business once they were installed. Jerry asked Mark to envision both products up and running in the business, then asked which product would offer better results. After Mark thought through the scenario, it became apparent which product was the best for his company. Jerry smiled and said, "Well done, Mark."

Asking discovery questions is a real art. It's hard, but it's needed to unleash the true power of the question. It requires one to disengage from the emotions of the situation, listen intently, resist the easy path of just blurting out what you're thinking, and crafting the right question creatively. But while it's hard work, there's a great payoff: enlightenment through self-discovery.

Lesson 25

Blow it up to Get it Right

W e live in a world that favors incremental improvements. We take what is and try to make it better; everything can be fixed or improved by a tweak here or a nudge there. Put a group together on a specific issue and the ideas will be endless. This is not a negative judgment on incremental change as it works in most situations, but at times you can't take what you have and make it right simply through incremental improvement.

Sometimes things need to be blown up to get them right. This means taking what's there and eliminating it, leaving a huge void. A void creates a blatant need, cultivating a sense of urgency to initiate action. The process will quickly identify who really cares and wants to put in the effort to make it right. Also, voids create a "clean slate" opportunity for creativity. There will no longer be things standing in the way that were done in the past, nor will there be legacies to live up to or special treatment to be protected.

Three factors are usually present when it's time to blow things up:

1. **There's a pattern of underperformance.** For months or years, incremental changes have been tried without success and the low performance is beginning to take its toll.

2. **Those involved are getting frustrated with the lack of success in improving the situation through incremental changes.** They still believe, though, that there's a knob out there that will raise the level of performance when adjusted.

3. **One or more sacred cows are involved and very few people realize their influence on the situation.** In fact, when considering changes in the past, these sacred cows were off limits.

For example, Dan found himself in a situation just like this. He was the VP of operations for a mid-size firm that sold products and consulting services to large businesses. Eight years ago, his firm paid a software company more than $1 million to develop a system that handled everything from order entry, to scheduling consultants, to invoicing, to product inventory. Senior management was very proud of the system and bragged about how much they spent to get a system designed specifically for their firm. The system was great at first, but as the business changed it never seemed to be able to hit the mark on subsequent releases. People never really complained outright; they just incorporated workarounds to get their jobs done.

Every two years, the software company presented Dan with a support contract. Each new contract would include the cost of upgrades to hardware and mid-tier software, as well as software modifications to their custom system. These contracts were getting more and more expensive and, upon receiving the last one, Dan decided it was time to get it right. He told his department and the software company that in six months, his firm would no longer use the software system because he was cancelling the contract.

Key players in the overall process approached him and asked what they would use in place of the old system. Dan told them he didn't know but they would have to figure it out before the end of the contract. Teams were formed, options were researched, budgets were established, a solution was selected, and an implementation schedule was developed. Within the six months, the firm was successfully using a slightly customized cloud-based application, costing them much less.

Lots of situations can be blown up to create a void. This applies to employees, processes, and tools. For example, employees who may have performed well in the past could wind up being less than stellar for some time. They may be well-liked and in highly prominent roles, but getting rid of them will free up others to assume more responsibility and express more ideas. Also, the processes you use to serve your customers are always ripe for replacement. Your employees may be comfortable with them and your customers may have liked what they got in the past, but that doesn't mean the processes are giving your customers exactly what they want or need right now.

There *is* one risk to blowing something up, though: It may not produce anything better. Here's one last piece of advice to minimize your risk: After blowing something up, don't have the first few steps of a new tool, process, or hiring procedure already designed in your head. It will take away the motivation and ownership of those who care and want to get it right.

Look out over your environment. Is there underperformance anywhere and are people getting frustrated? Are any sacred cows involved? It may be time for a big change.

Anyone got a match?

Lesson 26

Five Pillars of Practical Project Management

R eally? Just five? With such a preponderance of project management literature, it's hard to believe there are only five pillars of practices that project managers have to engage in to maximize their potential for success. OK. What are they?

1. Project Planning
2. Project Baseline
3. Reporting
4. Change Control
5. Project Closure

That's it. If project managers can do these five things, and the little things behind them, they will see great gains in project management performance and greatly enhance their ability to succeed. Sounds simple enough, but sometimes the simplest things are the hardest to accomplish.

1) Project Planning

Project managers need to stop over-complicating this initial phase. In its basic form, project planning focuses on identifying and documenting items related to a project's scope, time, and cost. In short, it's the basic process of documenting each party's understanding about the project.

Nothing else should be allowed to creep into this phase. The worst thing that happens at this stage is when project managers take a project plan and start adding little things to it. The project plan must be matched with the project's size and complexity, and tailored accordingly. It's not a "one size fits all" approach.

2) Project Baseline

The project baseline captures the project's predicted scope, time, and costs at the beginning stages, or anytime thereafter if someone chooses to change them. In other words, it's a snap of the chalk line. Project teams must treat the baseline as sacred, and only modify it through the change control process described below.

This is possibly one of the hardest things to get through to project managers, and once again culture is the culprit. If a company's culture is one in which people tear one another down when mistakes are made, then people are always going to hedge their bets. Nobody thinks what they've got is going to be good enough, and therefore they overestimate what can realistically be done. Project managers must become good at knowing when good enough is, well, good enough, and have the discipline to toe that line.

3) Reporting

Reports should be based on variances from the baseline in terms of time, cost, and scope, and they need to be metric-based to ensure people are collecting information on a regular basis. If metric-based reporting doesn't occur, then managers won't ever get the data they need because there's no driver or reason to collect it.

Good reporting ensures all people are collecting important information on a regular basis, and it keeps all project managers out of the fantasy world they so often like to inhabit. It keeps them anchored in reality. Most project managers don't like to report on progress, and yet somehow they continue to believe (i.e., hope) they will magically improve anyway. Reporting provides a snapshot of where project managers and their projects really are at any given time, not where people wish them to be.

4) Change Control

The change control process is meant to protect sacred project baselines while helping manage key expectations among project stakeholders. The very word "control" implies that, somehow, the process is intended to stop something from happening. But while change control needs to be a strict process that treats the project baseline as holy, it does not need to be inflexible. This is an important distinction that eludes many practitioners, much to the detriment of project results.

The main goal of the change control process should be to get and keep everyone on the same page, foster discussion, and then realign expectations when necessary. Rather than emphasize control per se, project teams should place more emphasis on collaboration. In other words, everyone needs to view projects with all three major criteria in mind – cost, scope, and time – since this is what leads to project success. If, for example, a change in time is requested, there will likely need to be some give and take in the other two areas to accommodate the request. When project managers are able to see the big picture, they're much more willing to compromise on certain issues if it means realizing a greater overall result.

Simply put, change should not be feared. However, stakeholders must understand that they can't get something for nothing. Instead of prohibiting any adjustments, the change control process should foster the free exchange of ideas, negotiation, collaboration, and a realignment of expectations. The process should not be a single-pass, "my way or the highway" process.. Rather, it requires multiple iterations and, often, relationships need to be nurtured to ensure the team finds the best possible solution to the change. This approach serves to remove ambiguity in expectations, and is the *only* process by which the hallowed baseline should be changed.

5) Project Closure

When one project finishes, there's always one or more needing to start, often behind schedule. Project closure is often skipped because of this to the detriment of everyone involved. Without closure between projects, work becomes a monotonous flow of never-ending intensity. Closure is important intellectually and emotionally. There's no hiding when a stakeholder is asked to sign off on projects; they either do it or continue the project. It forces finality. Lessons learned must then be collected to broaden the project team's and the organization's experiential base.

Finally, members of the project team should get together to enjoy each other's company, replay the good memories, and laugh at the not-so-fun ones. This builds emotional bonds between project members and encourages them to move on and embrace future challenges.

Don't underestimate the amount of effort it takes to master these five areas. They contain the bulk of project challenges and forgo the "nice to know" stuff. That's why the five pillars are so important. They keep project management practical and reap efficient success as a result.

Lesson 27

Three Tactics to Personal Growth

H ave you ever thought about how different you are now than you were five years ago? How about 10 years ago? You know in your head you have changed, but identifying the degree of that change is difficult. That's because you've changed slowly over time. Rarely in life do we encounter a significant event that drastically changes us and causes us to take notice. It's more likely that we take a slow, gradual journey to change, taking in life's ebbs and flows.

So what about personal growth? Are we bound to the same slow maturation process? Or, is there something we can do to cause ourselves to grow faster? The answer is, *yes, we can affect our personal growth rate.* Everyone knows kids grow much faster than adults do. That's because their environment varies significantly during their early years, causing them to acquire, adjust, and adapt to life. Cultivating our environment as adults is the key to personal growth.

Here are three tactics you can incorporate in your life to accelerate your personal growth:

1. **Associate with people better than yourself.** They will show you things you didn't know could be done, how they think and approach things, and what to avoid. Again, don't think there is going to be a big "A-ha!" moment with them. You'll absorb the

benefits over time through osmosis. The people you associate with don't have to be better than you in all areas of your life, just the ones you want to grow in. At work, it may be peers who are high performers. To find others, participate in local trade associations or online social groups. Find two to three mentors who are out of your league and meet with each of them twice a month. Take in their wisdom and criticisms, seasoning how you act and what you do.

2. **Put yourself in situations that make you uncomfortable.** Accept challenges. You'll find yourself in predicaments where you don't know what to do and have to figure it out. Challenges also steel your resolve and foster optimism through successes. Grapple with your fears and you'll develop coping mechanisms for managing them. With time, you'll also become callous to your fears and other risks. Delay immediate gratifications and learn to struggle now for a reward in the future. This will strengthen your discipline and perseverance. In addition, all these situations will give you new issues and questions to review with your mentors.

3. **Take in lots of diverse information.** Sure, go deep in areas you have a lot of interest in, but also learn broadly around the edges. History is filled with lessons about one subject becoming the catalyst for extreme growth in another subject. If you tend to enjoy the arts more, pursue science—and technology—related topics. If you enjoy sciences, learn about literary- and history-related topics. Read biographies to gain insights into how others thought about unique situations they found themselves in. Research different cultures to learn about how others think and how they developed their methods of thinking. When you come across something you don't know much about, research it on the web.

Personal growth is not for everyone. That seems odd to say; after all, who wouldn't want to grow personally? The issue is the cost of growing. Incorporating these three tactics into someone's life may cause them to lose control, feel unsafe, and exert effort. Lots of people don't want to go through that.

Everyone has to find their place in life. Those who want to grow, and can handle the costs of doing so, will have a fuller life as a result. It's not good or bad, right or wrong. It's just what they want to do. If that's your choice, grab hold of these tactics and take a ride. They may not be comfortable but they'll be a real adventure.

Lesson 28

Great Organizations Reward Prevention, Not Heroism

K illing alligators. Putting out fires. These are common phrases used in business to describe a person's workday. They sound macho, very accomplishing, and self-important. They denote a day spent fixing problems and resolving issues, but they're also a sure sign of an individual who works in an organization that rewards heroism.

In these organizations, there are the heroes and, as expected, the villains. The villain's sole purpose is to sustain the hero. They are either a person who caused the situation, or situations we get into in the chaotic world we live in, although people make a much better villain since they can be both attacked and shamed.

The problem with organizations that reward heroes is that they're not very productive. In these organizations, people are constantly on the lookout for villains who can catapult them into the role of hero. This uses up a good portion of an organization's capacity, leaving less energy to produce. The bottom line is that the organization's focus becomes being a hero versus fulfilling the organization's main role.

On the flip side, great organizations reward prevention. Prevention is all about destroying the matches that start the fires and removing the eggs that breed the alligators. These organizations operate under a philosophy that can be illustrated using the following analogy:

*At the beginning of the year, leaders of all organizations are given 50
gold pieces. They have two options available to them for using them:
They can invest by spending 40 of the pieces in the beginning of the year
to have a 95% chance that no problems will arise during the year. The
second option is to pay one gold coin for each problem that occurs during
the year with a 95% chance of them occurring.*

Great organizations would select the first option. Over time, they
will have vastly fewer problems or issues to resolve, leaving lots of
resources left to produce what the organization was intended to generate. And year after year, those resources accumulate.

Creating this type of organization requires a behavioral change in
its leader. He or she must first learn to welcome problems and issues
by not looking for the villain behind them. Instead of asking "Who
caused this?", they need to ask "How did this come to be?" This
encourages people to bring all the data to the forefront so it can be
analyzed to find the root cause. When problems or issues come up,
leaders need to tell people the organization is already getting better
because it has the opportunity to change and not allow the same thing
to happen again. By not highlighting the villains, the heroes won't get
the great reward and, accordingly, won't look for other villains.

Secondly, leaders must also be patient in making the changes to
resolve problems by not looking for the quick-and-easy solution. To
destroy matches that start the fires and remove the eggs that breed the
alligators, leaders have to promote **systems thinking**. The systems
thinking view of the world models the true nature of our organizations with many interconnected variables. It denounces the simple
linear "cause and effect" model that generates simple solutions today
that become problems tomorrow. Systems thinking can be learned,
but it takes time to incorporate it into our problem-solving process.
The best resource for bringing systems thinking to your business is
Pegasus Communications. (http://www.pegasuscom.com) They can
help organizations learn to think holistically.

These two actions can dramatically change your organization's level of performance. Imagine not having to worry about the plans you have for next week being derailed because of recurring problems or issues. Imagine what you could accomplish in a year when your strategy and plans take top priority and are not usurped by day-to-day operational demands. Life can be different when you reward prevention and not heroism.

Lesson 29

Working With Your Project Triangle's Flexibility

W e've talked about how useful the project triangle (Chapter 7) is for understanding the dynamics between scope, time, and cost on projects. Now we're going to see how useful it is in making decisions about controlling projects.

Every project is launched with an explicit or implied priority scheme for the project triangle. This priority scheme establishes which side of the project triangle is most flexible (lowest priority) and which is least flexible (highest priority) when it comes to leveraging one side to benefit another. In fact, all project planning efforts use a priority scheme to create the initial estimates of what's going to be built, how long it will take, and how much it will cost.

The majority of projects start with scope being the highest priority and, therefore, time or cost must flex to meet the demands of the scope. Sometimes the number of resources is limited, making time the most flexible; this is when the project end date is determined by planning efforts and not stakeholders. In other situations in which scope is the highest priority, the project's end date may need to fall within a 6-month window; this is when the number of resources and money need to be readily available to accommodate the scope and time.

Many different factors determine the priority scheme for projects. If the project deliverable is aimed at beating your competition to market, then time will be the highest priority. On these types of projects, cost will be identified as the most flexible side of the triangle. If the project is going to use an iterative methodology for development, there too, time will be the highest priority. Each iteration will be time-boxed to accommodate the development approach, and the number of resources will be held somewhat steady, forcing scope to flex the most. In tough economic times, cost will be the highest priority. This is also true of projects that are funded by grants. In each of these situations, scope will be the most flexible because there is usually a time frame in which the project needs to be completed.

It would be nice if priority schemes remained the same over the life of a project, but unfortunately, they don't. Some of the changes may be driven by external fluctuations in the business environment: economic cycles, competitor behavior, customer demands, etc. These *can* happen from time to time; however, the vast majority of priority changes happen because of the specific time in the project lifecycle: major intermediate milestones or project completion. For example, take a project with scope as the highest priority. As the project nears completion, the stakeholders often become impatient and want the major deliverables sooner than later. Now, all of a sudden, time is the least flexible and cost is the most. In iterative developments, as the stakeholders come to the end of the time-box, it may be most beneficial to make scope the least flexible and time the most. This is because it may take longer to pull out features than to keep them in and finish them late.

Decisions made on projects based on priority schemes usually are critical in nature. For this reason they need to be explicitly agreed upon and communicated. When the project is being planned there should be an agreement with stakeholders about which side of the triangle is the most flexible and which is the least. Remember, as the project progresses, the prioritization can change. It's not as though there is a specific point in time when the prioritization scheme changes; it's usually discovered over the course of many decisions. But when it becomes clear, the recognized change needs to be agreed to and communicated among all project stakeholders. As with all projects, the more clarity people have regarding the project's environment, the more consensus you'll have when making decisions and the quicker the project will be completed.

Lesson 30

People Want to Do Good, BUT...

I know you have lots of reasons to not believe this, but people are good. They care about others and want to help those in need. Yes, yes, there are some rotten people out there, but their percentage is much lower than you think. Most people know the difference between what's good and bad, have reasonable levels of empathy, and a disposition toward the betterment of others.

Remember how people responded after 9/11 by contributing hundreds of dollars each to individuals hurt or killed, by giving Hurricane Katrina refugees shelter in states all over the nation, or when thousands of volunteers sought tirelessly for weeks to find Elizabeth Smart when she was missing? They saw a need and chose to do good for the benefit of others.

The problem is, these examples are the exception and not the norm. It's the big BUT hanging out there that leaves us wondering: **Why don't people do good even though they see opportunities that would cause them to *want* to do good?** Before we get to the reasons of why people act this way, we need to know why it's important to address this topic from a business perspective. Individual goodness and kindness create a work environment that fosters productivity and job satisfaction. This is job one of a manager. There's no disputing the outcomes wanted and the results generated; it's something a leader has to pay attention to.

There are two reasons why people do not consistently do good, and both have to do with their environment. The first is that their environment **preoccupies and overwhelms them, drowning out the good they want to do.**

For example, Ed had been his division's new director for about four months when he was invited to attend a two-week executive education program at a major university. Upon his return, he had a lot of ideas to make his division different. Most of them were related to how he would engage and motivate employees at work. People became excited as he shared his ideas with them the week after his return, but they soon became disappointed as Ed went back to his old self, working long hours, giving people limited attention, and passing quick judgment on others followed by cutting remarks. Ed was back in his old environment, acting in his old ways again.

Every one of us has spent many idle hours on long car rides or days on vacation, and thought about the good things we should do for others when we get home. Upon our return, those ideas seemed to drift away. What stopped us from acting on them? We went back to our normal life routines and our good intentions got pushed out.

The second reason why people don't consistently do good is that **their environment rewards them to misrepresent their true desires.**

We all know someone at work who is seen as callous and seeks achievement at the expense of others, only to hear from friends in common how nice and good the person is in a non-work environment. We're often left in disbelief, thinking they live a double life. The truth is they do. Their work environment requires them to act insensitively in order to survive and prosper, but their true selves come out at home, where they want to do good for others. If they want to have a good career and provide for their families, unkind behavior in the workplace is what is rewarded.

At this point you may be thinking: How do I, as a manger, help these people change their ways? The answer is that we address these same issues in ourselves and model the behavior others will want to follow. This will give us insight into how to change and how to enable others to do so.

So what do you need to do differently? Regarding the first environmental issue, you may not be able to prevent yourself from getting overwhelmed and preoccupied in your job, but you can establish firm boundaries or rules to help you break loose and do good when you're aware of the need. Here are four examples:

1. If someone comes into your office or cubicle and asks you a question while you're working on something, push yourself away from your desk and give them your full attention.
2. If there is a death in the family of someone you know, go to the funeral.
3. If a person or a member of their immediate family has a tragedy or is severely ill, send them flowers.
4. If someone appears to have done something wrong, ask them to explain what they were thinking and why they did what they did before you pass judgment.

Every person has a different set of weaknesses regarding their display of kindness. Each person's rules and boundaries will be different as a result. Encourage others to seek and identify them in their own lives to get the good out.

Regarding the second environmental issue, it's much more difficult to counteract an environment that rewards behavior that does not produce good. It requires us to review our morals and practice a lot of internal dialog before we can establish a clear set of actions. Change usually occurs after a watershed event or long nights of questioning. Once you untangle yourself from your spider web, you'll be better able to help others get out of theirs too.

When everything is weighted on the scales of good or bad, the things that preoccupy us or cause us to behave contrary to how we want have little to do with the legacy we wish to leave behind. In reality, being known for doing good for others is much more powerful than what we actually accomplish in life.

Lesson 31

Seven Ground Rules for Every Project Stakeholder

Most projects start off with low levels of stress and lots of congeniality. Meetings are filled with give-and-take where people are amenable to differing views and approaches. How nice. But when the project gets underway and things don't progress exactly as planned, stress levels start to increase and meetings become confrontational. Stakeholders become much less amenable to others' contributions and very protective of their interests.

Alex, for example, experienced this in spades. When his project encountered several jolts of misfortune, he found himself attending one contentious meeting after another. It was now clear that Ed, who was representing the end-user group, had a different view of what was to be delivered. He wanted what he thought he signed off on, and when it was promised. Ed didn't care how much overtime or additional resources it required. Ginny was the line manager for a good portion of the resources that were matrixed into the project team. She had assigned some additional resources to the project to help it end on time, but her department was now stretched too thin. Ginny was counting on her staff to complete the projects by the scheduled date and didn't care how it impacted the project's deliverables. Pam, the project sponsor, had an approved budget and no reserves left since the company was nearing the end of its fiscal year. She also didn't have much energy for negotiating with the other project stakeholders. Alex knew that if no one budged from their current position, the project would end at some point and deliver something, but wouldn't please anyone.

When stakeholders participate in building the project plan, they're very aware of the project triangle and its need to be harmonized. As work on the project begins and things start going awry, stakeholders often grab onto the side of the triangle that holds their interest, and then begin to defend their position at the expense of the other stakeholders. From the above example, you can see that end users tend to care about scope and time, resource managers care about time and cost, sponsors care about scope and budget, and project managers— of course—are concerned with all three sides of the triangle.

When the interests of the stakeholders are polarized and the stakeholders ignore all sides of the project triangle, no one gets what they want. Communication deteriorates and is only present when there is overwhelmingly bad news. People confront each other, become offended, and establish grudges. In the end, the project finishes abruptly, producing a crippled deliverable, and a failure in everyone's eyes.

What's needed is **a way to take the behavior demonstrated by stakeholders in the beginning of a project and carrying it through to the end**: a mechanism for keeping stakeholders in lock step with the project manager. What's also needed is **a set of project tenets that everyone understands, agrees to, and reflects on continuously throughout the life of the project**. This practice has worked time and time again but has received little attention in the project management community.

For a project to have a chance at success, stakeholders have to understand the following seven tenets:

1. Projects are complex and have many variables that can cause a project to go off plan; change is going to happen.

2. The project triangle is real and must be continuously harmonized.

3. Scope is precious and should be handled with care since that's what will bring value to the company.

4. Scope always has ambiguity, and it's everyone's responsibility to collectively resolve and eliminate it.

5. Project team resources are finite and extremely valuable to other projects in the organization.

6. Costs are finite with defined limits.

7. Time can be manipulated, but not radically reduced.

Project managers who use these tenets include them in their project plans. Some also have them laminated and ask stakeholders to pin them on their walls. But the most important action project managers can take is reviewing the tenets monthly in status meetings and identifying circumstances and behaviors that are consistent and inconsistent with them.

Not all stakeholders will like the seven tenets though. A few will think they're goofy. Others will think too much emphasis is being put on securing future excuses rather than working hard to deliver on what was promised. But, most will appreciate them. In the end the tenets will be remembered and kept in mind when things get tough.

A word of caution: Project tenets are not foolproof. Projects still involve people and their uncontrollable behavior. However, tenets do provide a better shot of seeing more of Dr. Jekyll and less of Mr. Hyde.

Lesson 32

Sometimes the Process is Just as Important as the Product

R esults matter and should be the aim of every employee. Achieving results is what differentiates good employees from great ones. Sometimes though, when the result being pursued is a product or deliverable, the process used to deliver that result needs the same level of attention as the product itself. In other words, **sometimes the process is just as important as the product.**

Process is how you go about getting things done, how you achieve results. Process is especially important when the product being produced requires buy-in from a group of people in order for it to be a success. Examples of this are when a change is required in how people do their work, an organization's structure, a company's strategy, and who gets hired. In these situations, it may only take a few people to design the change and announce it, but if the people who are impacted by the change don't get the opportunity to influence the design or voice their opinions, they'll blatantly rebel against the change when it's implemented, or act passive aggressively and undermine its success.

Jason, for example, experienced this as the manager of a medium-sized department that processes customer service requests for an online product distributor. The volume of transactions was reaching the point at which the department's response goals were being missed regularly. Customer service requests were being processed without any filtering or routing. That meant that every team of processors had to know how to handle all the different flavors of requests.

Jason decided to change the way the department processed the requests by dividing the requests into three different types and using a filtering and routing process so the newly formed teams could specialize and gain efficiencies by focusing on one type of request. Jason selected three out of the five team leads to join him in designing the new process and team structure. They worked hard on it for four weeks, then announced the new structure to the rest of the department.

The two team leads who were not asked to participate in the change became extremely angry and threatened to quit. The rest of the department didn't like the change because they enjoyed the diversity of requests and were afraid they would become bored in their jobs. Jason listened to the feedback but went ahead with the changes. After six weeks under the new approach the total number of transactions processed was less than what they were before the change. One of the old team leads left the department and, with him, a major source of knowledge related to one of the types of customer service requests. To top it off, Jason's boss was noticing the department's poor performance and was putting pressure on him to fix it.

Clearly, Jason needed to put more emphasis on how he produced his results, but what could that have looked like? Before we go there, let's understand why people choose not to put as much attention on the process as they do on the product. It's because it causes the project to take at least twice the amount of time to get to the end result and it brings out emotions earlier in the process that are not very fun to deal with. No one in their right mind would choose this path if it wasn't needed. But sometimes, to have a more successful product result, this is exactly what has to be done.

Here are three things you need to do to be successful in these situations:

1. **Identify all the people who have a vested interest in the change.** These are the folks who will be affected by the change and care about what happens.

2. **Clearly state the reason changes must be made and present it to the group**. The reason must be compelling and clearly evident that the status quo cannot continue. If you can't articulate the reason in a powerful way, then maybe the change is not needed.

3. **Present the group with a rough idea of the change you're thinking about and then facilitate a process for the group to give you feedback.** You'll most likely get some input you had not thought about that will make your ideas better. Even if you don't, at least you gave the group a chance to be heard. Also, when you ask for the feedback, make sure you tell them what you'll do with the feedback so they know it will be collected and processed appropriately.

As I said earlier, doing these things will make it take at least twice as long to get to the end result and will bring out people's angst. But that's still a much better situation than not doing them and having to deal with a much bigger wave of angst, and increasing the chances for people to sabotage any chance of success.

Lesson 33

Is Your Project Schedule Dynamic?

Most everyone starts their project with a schedule. At varying levels of detail, they define the work that needs to be completed in the form of tasks. Then, they identify the duration of each task and sequence them based on interdependencies. They may also associate the level of effort (hours) to each task. When all is said and done, they have a schedule that gives them the overall duration of the project and maybe the total level of effort needed for it. Great! There's nothing better than having a good plan at the start of a project.

However, no sooner than the first week of the project something happens: Things don't go as planned. Some tasks that were to finish that week didn't, and some that were supposed to take all week finished early, allowing for other tasks to start that weren't scheduled to start until next week. So much for a good plan. Now we have a schedule that doesn't reflect reality.

There's nothing unusual about this situation. It happens to every project. But one of the things that separates the good project managers from the bad project managers is how dynamic their project schedules are.

As work begins on projects, actual to date task updates are recorded and estimate to complete are re-evaluated for some subset of tasks. This often results in a change to the initial predictions; however, these changes may or may not be realized in a timely fashion depending on how dynamic the schedule is. Knowing the true current status of a project is paramount to delivering it close to the initial time, cost and scope predictions. It all depends on the frequency of the updates (actual to date and estimate to complete) and the underlying structure of the schedule.

Highly dynamic schedules are always built using the full functionality of a project management software tool, such as Microsoft Project. There's just no way to get around it. Managing the current status of all the tasks, maintaining the task interdependencies, and calculating the estimated completion date each week can only be accomplished with these tools. When updates are only accounted for once or twice a month and the underlying structure of the schedule is in the project manager's head, then scheduled updates will be infrequent and won't often reflect reality.

This is what Kevin, for example, experienced when he was asked by the CIO of a Fortune 100 company to audit an ongoing $20 million project to overhaul the company's financial applications. He began the audit by interviewing the project sponsors, program manager and project managers. The general feeling he got was that the project was progressing well but was a little behind schedule. After his interview with the program manager, Jessica, he asked if he could get a copy of her schedule. Jessica said he could and asked if he wanted it in the standard format. Kevin then asked what the standard format was. Jessica led him to the break room and pointed to a large 4-foot by 8-foot six-phase Gantt chart with a version date of seven weeks earlier. Kevin's stomach sank as he realized the audit wasn't going to go very well.

Small and simple projects can be effectively managed in the heads of the project managers using a Microsoft Excel spreadsheet to record major milestone dates. But don't try this with larger, more complex projects. It will lead to major surprises, lots of bad news, and missed opportunities. Build your schedules using a highly dynamic underlying structure and you'll save yourself time and a lot of headaches.

Lesson 34

Don't Ask for Permission When Forgiveness is Easier

You've heard it said that electricity follows the path of least resistance, so why shouldn't this principle apply to our decision making too? We've all been faced with making decisions in situations in which the time available to make the decision is less than ideal. In some of those situations, the best action was not readily apparent, causing us to seek permission or validation before we decide. Others had readily apparent actions but the time required to obtain permission came close to extending past the deadline for action. We can still remember the angst of the moment that caused us to freeze up when we decided what to do in the little time we had left to decide and had to choose between waiting for permission or just going ahead.

Next time you find yourself in one of these situations, ask yourself these two questions:

1. Is my motivation and intent pure in taking the action?
2. Is it easier to ask for forgiveness later than seek permission now?

Doing this will lessen the anxiety in making the decision and put you in the best light after the action is taken.

Let's look at two scenarios and see how asking these questions would help:

Scenario 1

Alison was the last one from her team in the office. They had released a new version of the order entry application for the sales department the night before and all had gone well. Her boss was currently in flight on a trip halfway around the world when the VP of sales came into her area. He was irate that one of his salespersons could not enter a huge order into the system. The customer wanted it booked today so it would fall into the current quarter's budget since he had no budget for it in the upcoming quarter. Alison researched the problem and found the error in the code. It wasn't hard to fix; however, her boss and department relied on a strict testing and configuration control process to ensure the quality of the application. The process required a set of regression tests and her boss to sign off on the new release before it was installed. This process would consume most of that night and the next day to complete. If Alison implemented the fix without getting permission, would her motivation and intent be pure? Yes, she wanted to fix the application so the company would land the big sale. Would it be harder for her to get permission for the fix than to ask for forgiveness the next day? Yes, since getting permission was almost impossible and putting in the fix had little room for failure.

Scenario 2

Mark wanted to take the direct flight next week on his sales trip. It was Friday and he was waiting for his customer to confirm the date and time of the meeting, so he had not booked his flight yet. His boss had left earlier for an extended weekend vacation, but was available via cell phone. When the customer confirmed the meeting, Mark checked the availability and pricing of flights and found that the non-stop flight was twice the cost of the connecting flight. Company policy required Mark to get approval from his manager before booking the more expensive flight. If Mark booked the direct flight, would his motivation and intent be pure? No, he wanted the direct flight regardless of the cost. Would it be harder to get permission than ask forgiveness when the airfare was reviewed? No, his manager was available via cell phone all weekend.

Next time, relax a little when you find yourself in one of these situations. Ask the two questions and answer them honestly. It may do you more good than harm to break the rules.

Lesson 35

Consistency is the Answer

I t's not uncommon for a business leader to think that his or her organization's performance is subpar when compared with similar organizations in other companies. They feel that others must be much more sophisticated and produce far better results. While these *feelings* may be true, the reality is far from it. As with most things in life, the distribution of performance follows the bell curve. A small percentage of organizations are spectacular and another small percentage are complete failures. The rest? Well, they're smack dab in the middle, not great, not bad, just good.

There's nothing wrong with being good, but when most leaders think about where they want their organizations to be, they set their sights on being great. And it's common for them to believe that the quality of their people is the biggest impediment holding them back. If they could just hire the best people, they would be much further down the road to being a great organization.

On the surface, this seems to be a realistic plan but if you take a step back and look at the big picture, the plan begins to crumble. Assuming that people's performance follows a bell curve too, there are only so many "best" people in the work force; the majority are average performers. No one organization can afford or entice all the best people to work for them. Therefore, the path to becoming a great organization must follow a different direction.

In athletics, they say that on any given day, any team or individual can beat any other team or individual. What that means is the talent, or raw potential, of any individual or team at the same level of competition is not the overall deciding factor in winning. All professional scouts, coaches and players know that what makes great players and teams is the ability to take the raw potential they have and consistently perform at the required level to win. In sports, there are individuals with great raw talent who can only intermittently perform as needed to win, and there are others with less raw talent who have found a way to consistently perform.

So the question that needs to be asked is: **"How does an organization take the raw talent it has in its people and consistently perform at high levels of achievement?"** The answer: The same way athletic teams and individuals do.

Know how you're performing. Don't guess, don't generalize, just track your performance and find out exactly how you're doing. What this does is help you establish a range of good performance. If you can compare that range to industry standards, that would be even better. Professional baseball players know that if they hit over .300, they're doing really well. That means they get three hits out of every 10 at bats. The last five World Series winners averaged a winning percentage of .583. Teams can only know these statistics if they track them. So track your organizational performance; you may be better off than you think. Then publicize it to all your employees. Keep it top of mind for them.

Also, know the best practices that are related to the functions your organization performs. Research it on the web or bring in consultants. You have to know what's possible. Then, you can develop a common language around each function. Standardize the way functions are to be performed and identify checkpoints that tell you if you're following the standards or straying from them. Baseball pitchers have checkpoints in their windups that tell them if they're off or not. That helps them correct while in the windup or in the middle of an inning. They have a common lingo with other pitchers that facilitates communication when corrections are needed. They use terms like "stay within yourself", "you're rushing" and "get on top of the ball".

Finally, cycle through the experience, observe, and refine loop as many times as possible. Managers need to be coaches to their employees. They need to help employees break down their functions into smaller components to work on them independently to get better. Use peer reviews on actual experiences to enhance learning opportunities for everyone. Hitters have drills that help them with each component of their swing. Coaches tape them in games and batting practices to facilitate the "experience, observe, and refine" loop. Coaches and players watch them together to gain input. No one gets beat up. There's only constructive criticism and the desire to help each other get better.

For the most part, you have the right talent to be a great organization. Yeah, you may need to exchange out a few bad performers, but the most important thing is to take what you've got and raise the level of consistency in your organizational performance. People will notice. It's a great reputation to have.

Lesson 36

How to Pop a Change Bubble

The FUD factor: **Fear, Uncertainty and Doubt**. It affects everyone in one way or another. Some get paralyzed by it and others get a rush of excitement. Nowhere is this truer in our lives than in how we deal with change, especially when it's forced on us and out of our control. It can be a change in employment, additional responsibilities, a new way of doing things, or different people to work with.

When we don't view a change as favorable and our FUD factor is running way above average, we usually respond by initiating some defenses. These defenses range from denying that the change is present, minimizing its existence, avoiding interaction with it, or eliminating it all together. Another way of looking at these responses is to visualize the person confronted with the change creating a bubble around themselves that insulates them from having to embrace and assimilate the change. These bubbles can be really thick and difficult to pop. In addition, they're unique to each individual because of the person's ability to handle the FUD factor.

There has been a lot written on how to prepare people for change and how a person going through change can deal with it better, but little has been written to help a manager get his employees to deal with a change so the business can move forward. This is a real issue. When a person's change bubble cannot be minimized through preparation, and isn't popped by the individual going through the change, a manager must find a way to assist with the popping.

Popping the bubble involves embracing and assimilating the change. These are two distinct phases that have to be dealt with when popping a difficult change bubble. A person embraces a change when they realize that it exists and is not going away even in the slightest manner. People assimilate a change when they take the first few steps toward living with it.

There are two things a manager must do simultaneously to get the bubble popped. The first is to **constrain the environment** of the person with the bubble so they *have* to embrace the change. This may mean establishing specific standards of performance, denying them access or involvement in certain aspects of their job, and changing where or when they work. The goal of any constraint is to remove distractions that might take the attention from embracing the change.

Let's look at Karen as an example. She, along with the rest of the project managers in her company, went through three days of project management training. When she returned to her job on Monday, Jim, her manager, announced a new standard of practice for all project managers. At the end of the planning phase of a project, a time-and-cost baseline would have to be established and used as a comparison to all actual time and cost data from that point. Karen didn't like this because she knew there would be variances between the baseline and actuals on her projects in the future. She had lots of anxiety related to this and Jim understood it. He told her repeatedly that everyone would have variances and no one would be judged on them until they had enough data to set a standard. Regardless, Karen still would not baseline her current project. Finally, Jim told her she would have to work in his office the next day and do nothing else other than produce and deliver the baseline. It literally took Karen all day to complete the task even though the act itself took only 10 minutes.

The second thing a manager must do is **offer motivation for assimilating the change**. This could be additional time off from work, gifts that align with the employee's interests, or personal favors granted by the manager. Don't be afraid to think outside the box and be way over the top. Taking the first few steps in living the change can be very tough and require extra special incentives. The goal of the motivation should be to illustrate how important it is to live the change and how much the manager wants the person to do so.

Let's go back to Karen: Jim offered her two tickets to a theatrical production she wanted to see and babysitting services to be performed by Jim and his wife if she baselined the project by the end of the day. In Karen's case, this one-two punch worked and got the results Jim was looking for.

You may think this is a lot to go through to get a person to embrace and assimilate a change, especially when others might have done so with little concern. There is some truth in this, but if the person is a strong performer and valued by the organization, a little bit of situational leadership is warranted.

Lesson 37

Three Actions to Ensure Your Vision Becomes a Reality

If you're a leader you have a vision. There are no ifs, ands, or buts about it. Your vision is the starting point to make your organization better in some way. It's supposed to bring about positive change and consumes a sizable portion of your organization's resources in doing so. But we all know that not all visions become realities. They start with such flair but can burn out before they're achieved. Making your vision become a reality is what separates the great leaders from the good ones.

If you want to ensure that your vision becoming a reality, take these three actions:

1) Don't Try to Boil the Ocean

Visions always have a lot of passion and desire built into them by their creators. There are no limits to the creative process and, as such, visions can become massive in scope. This is not a good thing. The larger the scope of the vision, the less chance it will become reality. The reason for this is that the bigger the vision, the more people need to be involved, and the harder it is to communicate the vision with clarity. Additionally, it will take more time to complete and thus, harder to keep the momentum moving in the right direction. In general, a vision should take no more than 18 months to complete; that's far enough over the horizon to constitute a vision and yet still very manageable. The vision should also have very hard edges, meaning you have to know what's included in the vision and what's not. This will become very important in the next action. Lastly, it should be very easy to communicate the vision to others; people should be able to follow the flow of the vision and easily connect the dots.

2) Learn to Say No in Lots of Different Ways

Visions put today in the context of tomorrow. This is not to be taken literally but figuratively. Because of this, not doing the right thing today will take you away from where you're trying to go tomorrow: achieving your vision. Visions rarely get derailed due to large unexpected events; they typically fail because they lose momentum due to attention and resource "parasite attacks" over time from other projects. Visions must be protected and, to successfully achieve a vision, leaders need to spend twice the amount of time *defending* the vision as they did creating it. This means saying no to people and ideas that appear to be great opportunities in the moment but will actually dilute the efforts directed toward your vision. Yes, these new ideas may make a lot of sense and can be easily completed in a very short time, but it will be at the expense of the vision. Leaders must become masters of disappointing people at a pace they can handle so as to not discourage them from pursuing your vision.

3) Hitch Yourself to the Initiatives

Initiatives are used to organize the efforts required to turn visions into reality. Leaders almost always delegate responsibility for managing these initiatives to their staffs. It's how organizations function and how work gets done, but not all work is created equally. Rarely does a vision consume all of an organization's resources. Therefore, there will always be projects commencing at any given point in time that have nothing to do with the vision. While it may not be efficient for leaders to get actively involved in these projects, it's imperative that they get involved in the initiatives of the vision. This tactic does multiple things. First, it shows others the level of importance of the initiatives and helps them prioritize their work accordingly. Also, if the momentum begins to drop, leaders will know it right away and be able to adjust the level of intensity to correct the problem. Lastly, leaders' level of knowledge and awareness related to the initiatives will be high enough to allow them to make real-time adjustments to resolve what's unclear about the vision. This will save time and reduce any frustration team members may encounter.

As you can see, having a vision only gets you so far as a leader. Making that vision a reality requires some heavy lifting on your part, but doing so will put you in another league. Follow these three actions and you'll be on the trail to success.

Lesson 38

The Purpose of V1.0 is to Make a Great V2.0

What drove us to become the consumers we are today? We want everything right now and just the way we like it. For the most part, these expectations are met: faster this, more options in that, and everything cheaper.

Unfortunately, when we move into our work environment we also apply these same expectations to our internal projects that create new products or significantly overhaul existing ones. End users, subject matter experts, and project teams alike strive to create a perfect product right from the get go. "I need to add this," and "can we change that?" can be heard in project status reviews.

The problem this causes is that to push a product from 80% to near 100% of the wanted capabilities or desires requires a disproportionate amount of extra effort and time. Plus, the additions have a little bit of baggage that comes along with them:

- Often, they are the wants of one individual and not necessarily shared by the larger user base.
- They're enhancements or mitigations related to a projected reality that never materializes.
- They require modifying newly built components, exposing them to potential problems.

A better way to create a new product or significantly overhaul an existing one is to create a version 1.0 while having a plan for version 2.0. There are many reasons to pursue this strategy, with the best being that it's congruent with and efficiently leverages an end-user horizon line. End users have a good idea of the core requirements they want for a product. However, they tend to be vague with some of the finer details and only become clear about them after they begin interacting with the core product. Creating a product with 80% of the capabilities or desires gets it in end users' hands faster, thus providing value sooner than later. It also cultivates better requirements through experience for version 2.0 with less wasted effort and time.

For example, Apple's iTunes application has the lion's share of the market. It's amazing and fun to use, but remember it started with a version 1.0 that was a rough diamond in the works. In fact, Apple purposely waited to introduce the iPod that took advantage of iTunes until version 2.0 was released. It's easy to not be aware of this since the initial version of iTunes was not as widely used as it is today. Our expectations as consumers are a little tainted because we tend to not be early adopters and only experience products that are mature.

Of course, not all products can afford to be less than the best when first created. Bridges, space satellites, and bulletproof vests have to do their jobs well on day one. But these are the exceptions. You may think this is also the case with conferences and training workshops. They may be one-time events for the participants, but because they do occur again in several months there's an opportunity to make a great version 2.0.

So, how do you change a person's mindset so they will accept an 80% version 1.0? You make sure they understand and experience the plan of how they will get to a great version 2.0. The plan has to involve:

- Version 1.0 having all the core requirements built out;
- Delivering version 1.0 on time to create value right away;

- A repository of detailed enhancements to be created and tracked; and
- Developing a schedule for version 2.0 before work on version 1.0 begins.

Once people experience the full cycle of a version 1.0 followed by a great version 2.0, they'll be much more open to it in the future. It really does lead to a better product in a shorter period of time with less wasted effort. Give it a try. There's really no downside to it.

Lesson 39

You are Not the Norm

It's fun to encounter different cultures, both within our country and outside it. Whether through travel or reading, we marvel at the differences and share them enthusiastically with our friends. When we travel abroad we look forward to experiencing others and come to expect the oddities. It actually makes our travel experience more invigorating and personal.

But, when it comes to our day-to-day lives, these differences can throw us off. They frustrate us and make life more difficult, causing us to say things like "I can't believe they thought that," or "Do they really enjoy doing that?", or "Why weren't they more concerned about what happened?", or "That's not how I would have done it." The root cause to all of this is our belief that we are the norm, the standard. We believe that anyone different from us is odd, lesser than, wrong, or bad.

Bluntly stated, though: You are not the norm. Your thought process is different from those of most people. Your background, lifestyle, political views, and religious beliefs are all different from those of most people. No matter how you see, do, say, perceive, or think about things, it's not necessarily the same for others. You're not always right, good, or better than others. You are who you are and they are who they are. Period.

So, why don't we naturally see ourselves not as the norm? Because we tend to associate and interact with people who are most similar to us. Our friends have the same level of education and affluence, type of profession, and involvement in various hobbies and activities. This lulls us into the simplistic view that everyone else is just like us, making life appear more predictable and causing us less anxiety and fear.

But the reality is there is no one right way, superior perspective, or dominant viewpoint. There is many of each and this is what we must tackle to become better in our professional lives. We don't need to change who we are, we just need to understand that others are different and that there are rewards in embracing this reality.

Take Eric, who was tasked with leading a project to provide an automated tool for a customer service process that was being done manually. This tool would be used by more than 100 customer service representatives in five different regions of the U.S. He had a handful of team members and a short deadline. Eric interviewed several customer service supervisors to understand the current process and felt he had a firm grasp on the details. His team began designing and building the tool, and he made several assumptions and decisions on behalf of the customer service reps. He felt he could do so because of his detailed knowledge and his proven ability to refine processes. The application was delivered on time and with very few bugs, but it's acceptance by the customer service reps was a complete failure. The assumptions and decisions he made on their behalf turned out to be completely incongruent with how they performed their work. As a result, the application did not assist them as required in their work environment. Had Eric not believed that his assumptions and decision for the customer service representatives were what most people would think and want, he would have pursued their opinions more aggressively and ultimately delivered a well-received product.

Not seeing ourselves as the norm and searching out what could be different from how we are will make us better professionals. We will build better products, manage others better, motivate others more effectively, be more tolerant of others, and be less surprised and frustrated when dealing with others. But it takes some work to get there.

To better understand and embrace others' differences, take the Myers-Briggs personality assessment test to understand yourself and others. Learn as much as possible about another profession that's much different from yours. Or, get involved in an association that has a diverse social and economic membership. Put yourself deep into other people's shoes related to a current event and try to understand how they feel and think thing about the situation.

All of this will expand your perspective and cause you to consider more intently how you see, think, and act in relation to others. You may even begin to realize there are just as may cultural peculiarities within your own country as there are outside it.

Lesson 40

Got a Strategy? You Need Portfolio Management

P utting a strategy together is very rewarding. Whether it's for your division, department, or small business, it gets you thinking about the future and all the possibilities. Hard work has brought your team to a point of consensuses, giving you a structured plan that has documented goals, objectives, and initiates. Now is the time for action.

Developing a strategy is hard; executing it is exponentially harder. That's because strategy, which is made up of future possibilities, has to merge with the day-to-day business environment, which is driven by immediate needs. Projects that are initiated from both realms compete for attention and recourses. It's a problem rooted in organizational priorities and resources capacity.

Many managers leave the decision of which projects are higher in priority to a subjective process. This almost always leads to the projects driven by immediate needs, those with inflated importance, that are given higher priority. This is because they tend to be related to keeping the business running smoothly. Strategic projects will never hurt you today; therefore, they receive a lower priority in the moment. Tomorrow always seems further off than it really is.

Here's an example: In the fall, Mike received his department's objectives for the upcoming year. They were key drivers in his company's strategy and his bonus was based on achieving them. He took his senior team off-site and identified a number of initiatives that would support the department's objectives. They also put together a timeline that included the specific launch date for a number of key projects to support the initiatives.

Spirits were high when his team returned to work the following week. The projects that were scheduled to start in the beginning of the year were launched as planned and progressed well. However, as the year went on, the remaining projects' start dates began to slip. Other work seemed to come out of nowhere: a client asked for unique customizations, an older product that rarely sold started receiving bad press and had to be upgraded, and an equipment recall came out that required a replacement to keep it under warranty.

When the year ended, only half of the department's objectives were met, so Mike received only a portion of his yearly bonus. It seems that Mike had reasons for not completing his department's objectives, but the reality is he had no basis for his decisions that either replaced or delayed the start of some projects.

Portfolio management helps ensure that projects with the highest value are completed ahead of the rest, while balancing an organization's capacity for work with the work it wants to complete. This requires knowing the overall value each project creates and what each project's unique priority is in relation to the others. That means being able to rank projects sequentially. (1, 2, 3, 4, etc.) This is crucial to being able to manage the workflow through the organization without overwhelming its resource capacity.

When you prioritize projects this way, some day-to-day business projects will be higher priority than strategic projects because not all strategic projects are of the highest priority to the organization. Also, the priority list is a living list: Projects get completed and drop from the list, new projects are added and placed ahead of other existing projects, and some projects will switch priority based on business circumstances.

What must hold true is that a lower-priority project can never receive resources ahead of a higher-priority project. If a high-priority project's completion date is slipping and requires resources to stay on schedule, the resources must be taken from a lower-priority project, which may need to be cancelled to allow a higher-priority project to start on time. These are hard decisions to make but it's the only way to do things to ensure your organization is balancing strategic needs with day-to-day business needs.

Going back to Mike's situation, customizing a product for a key client may be a high-priority project that scores ahead of a strategic project, but upgrading an older product that has rarely sold should not.

Incorporating a portfolio management process requires strategic thinking and discipline. The rewards will come in the future when you look back and see that what was once a possibility is now a reality. The rewards will also come in lessons learned where what seemed so imperative in the moment turned out to be a minor inconvenience in the end.

Successfully executing a strategy is exponentially harder than developing one. But incorporating portfolio management into your organizational processes is a necessity to turning a strategy into a reality.

Lesson 41

Baselines: A Valuable Tool in Life and Projects

We're all very familiar with baselines in life. We may not call them by that name, but they're all around us. They tell us when we should change the oil in our cars, how much we can afford to spend on vacation, how much our monthly payment is for our house, and what age our child needs to be to start school. Dictionaries define baselines as an imaginary line or standard by which things are measured or compared. That is why they're a valuable tool for us. They guide us and let us know if we get off course.

In projects, baselines are invaluable tools that help us navigate toward success. They're communication devices that establish expectations between parties: **When is the project going to finish? What is going to be delivered? How many hours of effort will it take to complete the project?** Yes, baselines are only estimates at the start of a project, but they also set the expectation that gets everyone on the same page. Baselines are often formalized in project charters and plans, requirements and design documents, schedules, and budgets. They're distributed broadly to establish a consistent set of expectations.

When baselines are compared to current progress and new estimates, they produce variances. These variances let us know how far off we are from where we want to be, signaling that we need to take strong action to get the project back on course. When these variances are monitored closely, they indicate trends that point to root causes of negative results.

Given that baselines are expectations among all project stakeholders, they need to be revered and protected. While it may seem like no big deal to quietly change some portion of the project baseline without letting everyone know, it destroys the trust and cohesiveness of all parties involved when it happens. Baselines should only be changed when approved by a configuration management process in which all stakeholders are informed of the desired change and its ramifications. This is not to say project baselines should not change; quite the opposite. Baselines *must* change. Very few projects are completed as based on their original estimates. Therefore, the expectations must be aligned closer to current reality as a project moves closer to completion. It's always better to be proactive and announce less than favorable news as soon as it's known than to delay it until it becomes a bigger problem and more of a surprise.

People struggle with project baselines in three ways:

1. They delay setting the baseline in the beginning until they get further along in the project so their estimates will be closer to what they actually deliver.
2. They keep their distribution limited and don't share their baselines broadly, leaving people in the dark.
3. They never change the baseline during the life of the project, which only disappoints stakeholders when the project is delivered.

At the root of these three scenarios is the fear that the baselines will hurt them. They're seen as a weapon to be avoided, not a valuable tool to be embraced.

Take Becky, for example. She was excited when she was assigned her first project to lead. It was a smaller project, but it was her chance to move into the role of project manager. Becky built her project plan and established a schedule. She had her team, boss, and project sponsor review it and, once approved, she began work. In the beginning, things progressed well and Becky was excited. One day her sponsor came to her office and told her he wanted to add one more item to the list of deliverables. She told him no problem, she would make it happen. A few weeks later, her sponsor came by again and told Becky he needed the project to be finished three weeks early. Again, because things were going so well, she thought she could meet his request. Then the project began hitting tough times. One of her key team members got sick and missed two weeks of work. Then she realized it would take twice as long to produce the extra deliverable the sponsor requested. Now Becky's schedule showed her finishing a month later than she first estimated, and almost two months after her sponsor wanted it finished. She told no one about the projected change in schedule and just hoped for a miracle. Becky felt that if she told her boss and the sponsor, she would never get another project to lead. For four months, Becky didn't tell anyone about how late the project would be delivered. When the expected date of delivery came, she finally broke down and told her boss and sponsor. They were shocked and surprised. Both of them explained they could have helped her if they had only known.

Becky stumbled in two major areas related to baselines: **She didn't treat the baseline as sacred**, and she changed it without going through the rigorous configuration control process. Changing scope or end dates always has an impact that must be understood and communicated. She also **failed to communicate the schedule variances and the need to align the baseline to the current state of the project**. As a result, Becky limited her ability to take corrective action.

The lesson here is that if we don't embrace the value of baselines it will not only diminish our effectiveness, it will handicap our project stakeholders and cause tough times for them. And nothing good comes when you have a surprised and disappointed stakeholder.

Lesson 42

Was your Project Late or Underestimated?

It's amazing how a simple tool such as a project schedule, with multiple tasks and a project completion date, can create so much shame or joy. Taken at face value, completed tasks and projects bring about strong emotional reactions. If the task or project is late, it's a bad thing. If it's early, it's a good thing. Very black or white. Quick judgments about the outcomes imply negative or positive behavior on the project manager or team member.

It's common to hear statements like, "The project manager must have been unorganized or did not work hard enough to keep his team on schedule." Or, "The business analyst really knows what she is doing, superior skill allowed her to finish the requirements document early." These judgments sound very cut and dried, but are they correct? Actually, they could be misplaced.

The problem with the above statements is they assume estimates are sound constants, and a person's skill, experience, and behavior are the only variables. The fact is, more often than not, estimates are flawed. If a project is completed late, perhaps the time required to complete the tasks or project was underestimated. Conversely, if a project is completed early, its duration could have been overestimated. Yes, behavior and skill do vary but no more than project schedule estimates do.

In reality, most estimates that are underestimated come from lack of experience or succumbing to management pressure. And, most estimates that are overestimated also come from lack of experience or risk-averse sandbagging during the estimation phase. Experience in estimating and the level of skills people possess only improve with time. But when all these factors are taken into consideration, a late task or project could simply be the result of management pressure, and an early task or project the result of sandbagging. Now, which person deserves the shame?

Next time you observe and assess a completed task or project, remember that you shouldn't judge the results at face value. **Dig deeper and look at the underlying circumstances, experience, behavior, and skill.** That's where the truth lies, and where just judgments are revealed.

Lesson 43

When has Documentation Ever Saved Your Butt?

We spend lots of time and energy covering our butts. Documents and emails are generated to record verbal agreements, records are created for tasks we work on, and emails are stored in elaborate folder structures. All this effort is put forth because we think we may need these documents in our defense later.

Before we get too far, let's describe documentation in more detail. There's a continuum of information that may or may not need to be documented. On one side, there are the obvious items that require formal documentation: contracts between a client company and their developer company, anything that establishes a project's scope baseline, or its modification, schedules, project charters and plans, etc. On the other side are things we would never think of documenting: The number of days in a month your boss wore his blue suit, how often you ate lunch at the office, how many times your cubicle mate went to the bathroom each week, etc.

In the middle are the gray areas that we have a choice to document or not document. These are the types of situations we'll address here.

So, how has this served us? When has documentation ever saved our butts? Yes, I'm sure there are a few of you raising your hands, but, how many of you didn't?

There are two courts where documentation can come to your aid: a court of law and a court of public opinion. You know what and where the court of law is. The court of public opinion is much different. It's comprised of your management, peers, team members, and anyone else who will listen to the gossip. It's conducted in hallways, lunchrooms, offices, and cubicles.

In the court of law, a large amount of money is spent creating contracts, agreements, and documentation. There's also a lot of money spent defending positions too. Opposing parties never agree on the interpretation of documents and what the circumstances of the situation behind the documents were. Countless hours are spent posturing and clarifying what was documented. This is not a problem if the price of losing a case is much greater than the legal costs of defending.

But what about the court of public opinion? Usually, money isn't spent or awarded, so money may not be at risk. But reputations are. The process is much less sequential and formal. Both parties share their documents and emails with managers, team members, and friends in an attempt to bolster their positions. Sometimes management meets to discuss the situation, but it results in very little resolution. It becomes a "he said, she said" situation. No verdict is proclaimed; neither party's reputation is seriously scarred, but a lot of time and energy is wasted.

Think about it. Where else could those hours have been used? What might have been produced with all that wasted effort? Given that we all have so much more work to do than we have time to do it, wouldn't it be better for us to tackle this other work than spend time protecting our butts? This is not to say we shouldn't keep any emails or document anything, we just need to be a little more reasonable about it.

Next time you start to document something, stop and think about not doing it. How much anxiety does this stir up inside you? This will give you a sense of how prone you are to wanting to protect yourself. Then, ask yourself if you're documenting to protect yourself or if you're attempting to enhance communication with the other party.

If you're enhancing communication, that's a good thing. Then, ask yourself what the potential consequences are if you don't document and judge the severity of the situation, with less of a bias toward risk aversion. In the end, it may not be worth your time and effort. All of these checkpoints may cause you to act differently. That's OK. Try it. It could be a very liberating experience.

Lesson 44

Match Your Medium with Your Message

W e've all experienced this: You address a personal issue with a colleague or you share critical information with a project sponsor and it blows up in your face. You had no idea it could have gone that way but it did, and now your relationship with that person is fractured. If you're like most people, you probably went over and over what was communicated, and can't figure out where it went wrong. Odds are it wasn't *what* was communicated but the *medium* you used to communicate it.

Today, we have many ways to communicate with others: face-to-face, videoconferencing, telephone, email, text messaging, fax, and snail mail. What you may not be aware of is that not all communication media are created equally.

The richest medium for communicating is face to face because it's made up of three elements:

Words account for 7% of the message, body language 55%, and tone of voice 38%. Correlate these elements and their importance with the different media above and you can see how they become less and less robust in communicating a message. Specifically, if you take face-to-face communication and insert technology into the mix for something like teleconferencing, it becomes a little degraded because of video resolution and sound quality. With telephone communication, body language has been removed, but there's still voice tone and words. Email, text messaging, fax, and snail mail are the leanest of the media because all you have are written words.

Add to this the fact that, with face-to-face communication, we have the opportunity to adjust our message in real-time based on feedback we're getting from the person we're talking to. If the person is giving us looks that indicate they don't understand what we're saying, we can elaborate on a point to clarify. If they appear to be getting upset, we can use softer and less direct words. This is another dimension to communication many of us don't think about. With speaking on the telephone we get some real-time feedback based on the other person's voice tone. But, with the written word (email, text messaging, and snail mail) there's no real-time feedback. It's basically a dump and run of information.

Every message you want to communicate has some level of volatility, and there's a chance that what you have to say will trigger the person emotionally and evoke a negative response. We're humans; we can't help it. That's why it makes sense to **match the volatility of the message with the communication media you have available to you**; meaning that the more volatile the message the richer the medium you should choose.

Sounds easy, but here's why we're unconsciously reluctant to do it. The richer the medium, the more we have to encounter uncomfortable feedback in the process of communicating volatile information. It's easy to hide behind email and say difficult things; and, it's hard to be more present and experience the uncomfortable feelings of communicating something volatile.

Take Susan, for example. She was managing a high-profile project that had just encountered a major technology hurdle that was going to delay the project several months and bump up the cost 15%. Instead of setting up a meeting to deliver the news face to face, she chose to send it out in an email, believing it would be more efficient. The response she got was very negative, as expected. But what she also got—which was not expected—was a firestorm of communication she could not control: accusations and recommendations from the original distribution list and many others up the chain of command. She was ultimately removed as the project lead, all because she did not deliver the news in a face-to-face meeting.

If you care about the relationship with the person you need to communicate volatile information to, or you need to control the response to it, invest the energy and follow the rule of matching the volatility of your message with the media available to you. It may be harder, but you have a better chance of getting through the difficult time with less negative impact.

Lesson 45

The Shortest Path to a Good Project Management Methodology

You look across your organization and see a wide variation between your good project managers and the weaker ones. Everyone seems to be doing their own thing and no one is taking advantage of your organization's best practices. You say to yourself, "If I only had a good project management methodology, I could raise the performance level of the weaker PMs by standardizing on best practices, plus everyone would know what to expect."

You're right! A good project management methodology will benefit your organization and its employees immensely. Performance levels of newbies and experienced PMs will rise, and supervising them will become a lot easier.

But deciding that you need a methodology is the easy part. Developing one or customizing an off-the-shelf version is a monumental challenge. As with all processes, identifying what data needs to be captured is fairly simple. Forms and templates can be easily created; in fact, this is usually where creators of project management methodologies start. They develop very detailed project charters, scope statements, project plans, work breakdown structures (WBS), change control forms, etc. However, this is also where the creators get jammed and leave out important parts of the methodology. During the majority of the project's lifecycle, with all forms and templates complete, PMs need to know what to do on Monday morning when they come into the office.

The day-to-day work is when PMs are faced with tasks that were supposed to start but didn't, tasks that were scheduled to be completed but needed more time, and new tasks that had to be added to the pile of existing ones. Because of all this, schedules must be revised to reflect new realities. Strategies and actions need to be developed to try and get the project back on track or more in line with the project triangle's flexibility guidelines. Plus, all the stakeholders will want to know the project's new status. This is where a cyclic routine is needed to provide some structure to the ad hoc nature of project management.

A project management methodology with lots of forms and templates that asks for the smallest level of useless detail will die a slow death and benefit no one. Project managers don't have an issue with rigorous methodologies as long as they're practical and beneficial. If all you give them is rigor and little help, then, come Monday morning, they will reject the methodology or put nonsense within the fields just to get through the process.

A first step in creating your organization's initial project management methodology should be to **hunt around for an off-the-shelf version**. Most likely it will be thorough enough for your initial draft, and if it's a popular one the initial kinks will already have been ironed out. Don't start with the Project Management Institute's (PMI) Project Management Body of Knowledge (PMBOK) though. It's far too detailed for the beginner and consists of a set of forms, templates, and job aids that don't have an integrated cyclic routine for the Monday morning PM. But try customizing it by cutting out anything that's not highly valuable. Instead of using a committee to do this, grab two or three star PMs and let them make the cutting decisions. Also, don't try and achieve perfection in one fell swoop; start by understanding that there will be numerous revisions in the two years after you adopt the methodology. Take the initial draft, use it for four months, and ask what could be better. Then revise it and go another four months and do the same. With every version, give multiple examples of what you're asking for. Don't leave the PMs wondering.

It's also imperative that you **select a project management software tool to standardize with**. No project management methodology can exist and grow on its own. Here again, start simple. Microsoft Project's single-user version is a great starting point. Use only the most valuable feature at first, then add others as time goes on. Major enhancements can be added later, even with components from vendors other than Microsoft.

As you move through the maturation process, you will begin to **integrate the software tools, forms, and templates into a nice cyclic routine**. Soon, you'll realize that not all projects need to follow the same level of rigor, leading you to declare that smaller projects don't need to follow this or that.

At this point, you'll have a rigorous methodology that provides tremendous value and you'll be able to say to yourself, "I have a good project management methodology and I'm raising the performance level of my PMs because I've standardized on best practices and know what's expected of everyone."

Wouldn't that be nice?

Lesson 46

To Confront or Not Confront

W e all have found ourselves in one or more situations in which we had to decide whether or not to confront someone. It could have been at the store when someone cut in line ahead of you, on a flight when someone was mistreating the flight attendant, or at the office when an employee's work was below par. There is no doubt your emotions were running high with anger and fear rushing through your body. Maybe you really struggled with the decision to confront, or maybe your emotions took control, causing you to automatically rush into the confrontation or withdraw from the situation entirely.

Very few people like confrontation. Most find themselves somewhere on the continuum between totally hating confrontation to dealing with it. A **good rule of thumb when deciding whether to confront is asking yourself if confronting the person will make a difference.** .Will the person learn from it or think twice before they display the same behavior? If not, then don't confront them. And especially, don't confront them when it only makes you feel better by giving them a piece of your mind. These situations always turn out bad. Either both persons' tempers get out of control, or you will emotionally unload on the person, leaving them startled, and you'll feel bad about it later.

When you choose to confront someone, make sure you use the least amount of emotion to get the effect you want. The person who is being confronted will always be somewhat defensive, and it's easier for someone to learn when they're the least defensive. Also, when the confrontation becomes overly emotional, know when to let go. For instance, if it's a person you don't know, there most likely won't be a lesson learned, so it's best for you to walk away. If you know the person, sometimes it's best to leave and live to fight another day. Going too far with this person can hurt your credibility and handicap your ability to make a difference with them in the future.

Lucy, for example, could have used some of this advice when she saw a man knock her son down while he rushed to the bathroom during a Little League game. The man was clearly not paying attention and didn't even stop after knocking down her son. Lucy was filled with rage and, after she picked her son up off the ground, rushed into the men's room. She confronted the man as he stood at the urinal, calling him every name in the book and demanding he apologize to her son right away. An argument ensued and he responded with a few choice words while zipping up his pants. Lucy left the men's room frustrated and embarrassed as bystanders stared and snickered at her. Not only did she feel bad about her actions that night, she became a disgraced legend in the league's circle.

So what do you do when you choose to not confront someone? Knowing that confronting the person will not make a difference will help you release the anger you feel in the moment and will help you disassociate from the situation. That's a good thing. But, what if you choose to not confront even when it will make a difference? This usually happens when you want to run from the confrontation because you hate it or find yourself feeling fearful. You may be saying to yourself the person will never learn, won't listen to me, or it's not worth it. But the real reason is you're overly uncomfortable in the situation even though you know confronting the person will make a difference.

Your feelings are real and valid, but you can choose to confront and act on them since you have many options available to you. If you don't have to confront the person right away and can do so later, then wait, but do it sooner rather than later. Delaying will allow you to calm your emotions and prepare your thoughts. A great tool in these situations is role-playing with someone. If you don't have the option of waiting, then ask someone to stand with you while you confront the person. This will give you strength. Just remind yourself that confronting a person when they mistreat you bolsters your self-esteem. When you do it to defend another person, you're carrying out a form of justice.

It's safe to say you will find yourself in many more situations in which you'll have to choose to confront or not confront. Yes, your emotions will be racing, but hopefully you'll ask yourself if it will make a difference and then make an honest decision. I bet that, most of the time, you'll find that the confrontation will go better than you thought it would.

Lesson 47

If You Want to Be Efficient, You Need Routine

E fficiency is a hot topic in the corporate world. Organizations are always striving to produce the most value for the least amount of effort. They attempt to embed it in their business models, strategy, and day-to-day operations. Unfortunately, they don't always succeed.

The major reason for this is that **organizations don't instill routine in conjunction with their efficiency efforts**. That's the difference between wanting and doing. Working harder will not get you there; working smarter will. Let's look at two examples of winning routines, then use them to extract the value and practices.

In the late 1990s and early 2000s, **Dell Computer** was in the middle of a huge pricing war in the computer industry. They and their competitors were slashing prices in an attempt to grab chunks of market share. Dell seized the moment by generating huge efficiencies in the sales and manufacturing functions of its business. Dell was the first to offer Internet sales and to allow the customer to configure the computer to his or her needs. Dell established manufacturing plants that, through processes and tools, were able to customize individual computers on a mass scale for less than standard costs. Because of these efficiencies, Dell drove many of its competitors out of business or to be sold at auctions.

Then, there's baseball Hall of Famer **Wade Boggs**. Most individuals have routines not because they're interested in efficiencies, but because they're familiar and comforting. Those who are interested in efficiencies are usually athletes, soldiers, or extremely high performers in business. Boggs played 18 years in the major leagues. He played in 12 All-Star Games, won a World Series, along with several Gold Glove awards for fielding and Silver Slugger awards for hitting. His highest honor was being inducted into the Baseball Hall of Fame in 2005. One does not maintain that level of performance over that many years without being efficient and having a routine. Each night before a game Wade would visualize four at-bats and imagine successfully getting four hits. He woke up at the same time every day, ate chicken before every game, fielded exactly 100 ground balls, took batting practice at 5:17, and ran sprints at 7:17. He drew the Hebrew word "Chai", meaning "life,", in the batter's box before each at-bat and his route to and from his position in the field was exactly the same each time.

So, what are the four key practices of winning routines? Here they are:

1. The first thing you need to understand is that **routines need competition.** You have to be able to keep score to know if your organization is winning or losing. Your opponent or industry benchmark standards may be your competitors. The score is kept based on performance in key areas and can always tell you if you're winning or losing.

2. **Routines must start at the top, be part of your organization's strategy, and work their way down through the organization.** Every process, tool, and employee must be directly tied to the organization's game plan for winning.

3. **You have to be intentional about the way you play the game.** Your organization must be able to describe what it does and how it does it. Processes have to be documented and habitually followed, discarding impurities along the way. Em-

ployees and their wages need to be continuously evaluated and reacted to. Low performers have to go away and wage scales must be established based on performance. The focus has to be greater production at lower cost.

4. **You have to be dedicated to your routine even when you're losing big time.** Your organization must be able to sustain its commitment through delayed gratification, knowing it will reap the rewards one day. There can be no quitting when things get hard or don't look so good.

Efficiency is a must for survival. You may not be concerned with it personally but your executive management and competitors are. If you don't pay attention to efficiency, they may come knocking on your door bearing bad news. Keep executive management and competitors at arm's length by instilling routine in your organization, and you may never hear that knock.

Lesson 48

Struggling to Define Project Approach?

It doesn't seem that hard to define a project's approach. It's just a description of the strategies for achieving the project objectives. Simply stated, it's the path the project team will take to get to the desired end result. Simple as it may be, it still drives many project managers nuts, causing them to stare at a blank page, unable to articulate anything of value.

Three types of project managers struggle with defining their project's approach:

- **Type 1:** Those who have always worked on similar projects.
- **Type 2:** Those who have worked on similar projects, but the conditions of the current project are not the same.
- **Type 3:** Those who have never taken on a similar project; neither have their organizations.

Type 1

Most industries have standard development approaches. Software development has the classic waterfall approach: requirements, design, development, test, and implement. In drug development, they are:

discovery and research, development, regulatory review, and approval. In construction: concept, design, drawings, construction, and commission. These standard approaches are not just detailed at the higher levels of a project; they're standardized deep into each phase.

As a result, most projects under normal conditions follow these standard approaches. It's no wonder project managers struggle documenting their projects' approaches with anything other than "do what we always do." This should be an acceptable phrase, one that can be used often. Let's stop thinking it needs to be anything other than that.

Type 2

When the project's conditions are anything other than normal, the project approach needs to be something other than the status quo. Here, project managers need to clearly identify what's different. Does the project need to be completed in an extremely shorter-than-usual time frame? Are the details of the end product extremely vague, and not because someone has not thought about it hard or long enough? Are there large risks to successfully delivering the end product?

Once the project manager knows the reasons for the variable conditions, they need to identify the flexibility they have with the end deliverable. Does it have to be delivered in one fell swoop or can it be developed through multiple "less than perfect" versions? Examples of the former are scheduling a conference, constructing a building, and building nuclear reactor control systems. Examples of the latter are creating websites, building consumer products, and developing certain software systems.

Another element to define in this situation is how important the project is to the organization. Does the organization's existence rely on the project's success? Will it be significantly hurt if the project is not completed successfully? Basically, the project manager needs to know how creative they can be in coming up with a viable approach.

Budgets and organizational resources are typically the main constraints to viable approaches.

With all these questions answered, the project manager can take their existing standard approach and decide how to change it to meet the challenges. One of the first areas to look at is how the end deliverable will be developed. If the project needs to be completed in a much shorter time frame than usual, a project manager may choose to initiate development phases that would normally be completed in series, in parallel. The contractor responsible for building the aquarium to save the star and orca in the movie *Free Willy* used this approach. The orca was going to die if he was not moved to a new facility by a specific time. The standard time for developing the facility had to be significantly reduced to meet the needed time frame.

If there are big technical risks, then using an iterative development scheme will eradicate the risks early in the project and allow for a more certain end result or quick project shutdown to save time for a different approach with a refined scope (also known as Plan B. Iterative development is also good for helping end users identify what they ultimately want by giving them a version of the product that grows in functionality over time. This approach is how Linux, the open source operating system, came to fruition.

If a project manager has a vast budget and resources, then experts and additional personnel can be acquired to ensure a successful completion. Y2K was a great example; companies had to get software converted by the end of 1999 and they pulled out all the stops to make sure it happened.

Type 3

Now let's address the project managers struggling to develop project approaches because they have just been given responsibility for a project of a kind they have never worked on before; nor has anyone else in their organizations. Obviously, there's a lack of knowledge and experience, but that's only the crux of the situation. It's not that the project manager isn't creative enough; they just don't know what they don't know and also don't know where to begin.

Thankfully in today's world we have tools that give us access to an enormously broad spectrum of information. Through search engines and bulletin boards, one can find out how others approached similar projects. Plus, with social networks, both personal and professional, help is just a post away. However, there's no silver bullet if project managers find themselves in this situation. They have to work hard and cast their nets wide to get the information and experience they're looking for.

Hopefully with the guidance given here, you'll know when to relax and not stress out about being strategically creative, have a roadmap for creating a strategy that meets your radical project conditions, and know when to become a sponge and soak up as much knowledge and other people's experience as you can to meet your new project's challenges. So, don't sweat it; it's really the strategy that will guide you to success.

Lesson 49

When Does Done Mean Done?

How many times have you asked someone to do something for you and, when they tell you they've done it, you come to find out it's really not done? It can happen when you're driving home after having your car repaired, opening the bag on a takeout order, or having your kids clean their rooms. The work was only partially completed or it's riddled with errors. Either way, it doesn't matter; done didn't mean done.

For managers, this is a real frustration. They end up playing the quality assurance role for someone else. Meanwhile, time is stolen from other things they needed to do. Managers want the work to be done right the first time.

Done means done when the end result matches the expectation of the requestor. Now we all know there's a lot to this statement: **Does the requestor know what they want and is the person responsible for the task capable of doing the work?** The majority of the time, the answer to these questions is "yes." So, what makes it so hard to do?

Basically, this is a work quality issue. No one sets out to screw things up, it just happens; and, usually because an employee was rushed for time, uninformed, or lacked an orientation to detail. While these can seem like reasonable excuses, they are not. They can all be overcome with some initial forethought and effort.

185

Employees shouldn't wait until the last minute to tackle a task. That way, they will have time to complete the entire task and review their work for errors without being rushed. They shouldn't play the victim role by saying "I wasn't told this" or "I didn't know about that" because their work missed the mark. They are responsible for finding out all the information needed to make sure their work matches the requestor's expectation. When assigned tasks, employees should use the 5 Ws to find out all there is to know: **Who** is going to use this information? **What** format is needed? **When** do you want it finished? **Where** is the data located? **Why** is this so important? Lastly, if an employee lacks an orientation to detail, they should have a co-worker review their work to uncover anything missing or in error. Everyone has strengths and weaknesses. Not having an orientation to detail is a common weakness, and having work reviewed by someone else is a great coping mechanism.

Take Jerry, for example. He called one of his new employees, Kelly, into his office to ask her to prepare a report. After telling her what he wanted, Kelly started asking a series of questions. Jerry was caught off-guard and a little bothered at first, but then realized Kelly was gathering what she needed to do the job. A week later the report was delivered on time and, after Jerry reviewed it, he was surprisingly amazed at the level of detail and completeness from someone so new to the organization. He called Kelly back into his office and asked her how she was able to do it. She replied that she developed the initial draft, then took it to two co-workers to review and they gave her a handful of suggestions that she incorporated. As Kelly was leaving Jerry's office, he smiled and thought to himself, "Wow! That's a great hire!"

Yes, making sure done means done takes extra effort and discipline, but doing it is what separates the great employees from the good ones.

Lesson 50

Shape Your Organization for Effective Change

N o organization is ever where a leader wants it; there is always something that needs to be different. In fact, this is a very healthy perspective. First of all, an organization needs to be different just to stay relevant. Secondly, all organizations have weaknesses; identifying and dealing with them is like working with fractals.

*[**Fractal:** a rough geometric shape. The closer you look at its borders, the more similar the variations in the borders are exposed. No matter how much you zoom in on the borders, they never become smooth.]*

Similarly, in your organization, the more weaknesses you see and fix, the more details you pay attention to, and the more weaknesses you find. This is the path of continuous improvement and Six Sigma.

Improving a process or product involves a cold version of change. The steps, functions, or capabilities are manipulated like a math equation to bring about different results, and it can happen very quickly. **But what about change that involves people, behaviors, and culture?** This type of change is much more personal and intimate; it requires shaping to bring about effective results.

Shaping can only originate from the leader of an organization. It requires their personal touch and investment to make it happen.

Let's look at what specifics you as a leader must know to shape your organization into a highly functioning one:

- **Shaping implies constant, gradual change.** If the right pace of change is not acquired, your chance of success is limited. Too much at one time will damage your organization due to fear and panic. Too little will not sustain change, causing your organization to adhere more to the status quo and ignore when change is necessary.
- **Because the change is going to take time, make sure you establish, in detail, a far-off vision for what you want your organization to look and act like.** Then detail small shavings of change that will act as stepping stones to your vision.
- **Each shaving needs a point person.** Most of you can delegate to your trusted staff, but some of you will need to execute on your own due to the importance or potential resistance within your organization.
- **As you begin to shape your organization, don't be surprised when your organization regresses.** Some changes have a strong memory and slowly revert back to the old ways. When this happens, put the required effort into getting things back in line and then keep your eye on them. Apply effort to ensure the change sticks.

As the leader, you're the only person who can keep your vision alive and keep your organization moving toward it. You have to be extremely diligent and disciplined. If you don't pay attention to it, your organization won't either. Your vision may atrophy and die as a result.

As I said earlier, when you decide to shape your organization, you're in it for the long haul. What will be fun for you is looking back at the end of each year and seeing that change does make a difference. Most people will not notice it like you will because it was a shaping process. That's OK, it's the different results you desired and will get credit for.

Lesson 51

Writing Good Requirements

W riting good requirements is frequently portrayed as a unique skill to business analysts. But it's not; it's a unique skill to good writers. Requirements are simply a condition or capability needed by a stakeholder (user) to solve a problem or achieve an objective. *Identifying* requirements is a unique skill to business analysts; however, writing good requirements has more to do with what you learned in high school English class. Remember your English teachers? They would spend a semester teaching you to know your topic, be thorough and concise, eliminate ambiguity, and organize your writing to create a smooth flow for the reader.

We all can relate to this story: Your teacher gives you an assignment to write a convincing article on a popular debate in current events. Your first draft is due next week, so you select and research a topic. You put the first draft together, review it, make changes several times, and hand it in. Your teacher reads it over the weekend and marks it up. She hands back the bloody red draft and asks you to address her comments. You can't believe she marked it up so much. You spend the next few days rewriting it and hand it in for another review, and it comes back with more red marks. You get incredibly frustrated. All you want is to be done with this assignment. You wish it wasn't so hard.

Times haven't changed much since high school. Many business analysts find it hard to write good requirements. When they're assigned to a project, there's a sense of excitement and anticipation. They start researching and interviewing stakeholders to find out what they need to be successful at their jobs. After compiling all the information, they begin writing the requirements. They work hard and put in a lot of hours, resulting in a cherished first draft. They send it out to the users and developers for review. When the comments start coming in, they feel hurt and frustrated. They make changes and send it out once more for review. Again, comments come back announcing dissatisfaction and more work. At this point, all a business analyst wants is to be done with this particular task.

If you can relate to this, it may be because you struggle with writing in general or you're a little rusty at it. Here's what makes a good set of requirements:

- First, **you have to know in detail what the problem and solution are.** You can't have a casual understanding. If you do, it will sink you for sure.
- Next, **each requirement needs to be specific and concise.** You're creating an image of the solution in the minds of your users and developers, one grain of sand at a time. Choose your words wisely; each one matters. Eliminate ambiguity by looking at what you've written from different points of view.
- Lastly, **organize your work so it flows smoothly for the reader.** You're taking them on a journey; there shouldn't be any holes in the image you're creating. Be thorough in describing all the facets of the solution.

If writing is not one of your strengths, work on it. Take a couple of English classes at a local college. You may not become John Grisham, but you'll get better. Besides, what gave you trouble in English classes when you were younger most likely won't be a problem. Life has a funny way of changing us without us even recognizing it.

Writing good requirements is hard and takes a lot of effort. It's much harder than any writing assignment you received in high school. Of course, the consequences of writing bad requirements are far greater than any you encountered in high school too.

Lesson 52

Get More Out of Life by Seeing the Shades of Gray

L ife presents us with so many different environments and situations. Each day, we pass judgments and take actions that help us navigate through our business, personal, political, and religious lives. We're continuously confronted with unprecedented amounts of information that can influence our decision-making process. While this is good in so many ways, it's also very exhausting. Decision making is hard because critical thinking is hard.

To escape this tiring predicament, we often establish biases or predispositions that help us select what information we take in and process and what information we ignore, deciding that what we ignore has little bearing on our previously established conclusions. In other words, we like to take in a little information, think about it, draw a conclusion and never reflect on it again. In the extreme, we make judgments that specific people, organizations, or things are always good or always bad; or, we establish specific principles that tell us to always do this or don't do that. Again, this behavior makes navigating through life easier.

The problem is that people, organizations, things, and actions are not always good or always bad. There is some amount of good in a bad organization and some amount of bad in a good person. In addition, no principle applies to all situations; everything is constantly changing and as a result, so is the degree of good and bad.

Now let's bring this into the real world. If you work in a business unit of a company, it's not appropriate to say your IT department is worthless. Nor should those in the IT department say Apple products are made exclusively for idiots. Republicans should not declare all Democrats are mindless and liberals should not say all conservatives are fascist. Your co-worker is not always lazy, your spouse is not perfect, and not everything your favorite celebrity does is fantastic.

You may not always adhere to your principles. You may decide to break the law or not donate to a charity. You may push away a loved one when they need you, or not fight back after taking a punch. You have lied to yourself in some way, and it will happen again.

Exiting early or never entering the critical-thinking process when you encounter a new situation or piece of information reduces your future possibilities or exposes you to additional risks. Why? Because if you ignore the new data and proceed with your predispositions, you're choosing to engage in the future with blinders on. Simply put, if you think Jim is always right and he tells you something that's flawed, then you're at risk. If Susan always over-exaggerates and tells you how beneficial something is, then you miss out. Not to mention, you may never learn anything new.

We have to constantly hold the tension of believing that, at any point in a situation, something or someone has the potential to be good or bad or present us with new and beneficial information. We have to engage the situation and stay in the critical-thinking process, all the while keeping an open mind. There are two things you can do to help in this:

1. When it comes to passing judgment, practice **cynical optimism**. Look for the good in what appears to be bad and the bad in what appears to be good. For example, every criticism

of you has good and bad in it, and every organization does some things well and others poorly.

2. When it comes to principles, practice **inquisitive protectionism**. Hold tight to your principles, but look for reasons for the situation to warrant a different action. It may truly be best for you and others if you do.

There is actually a lot of gray in this world if you look for it. It makes life a lot more interesting, attractive, and unexpected. Remember, all you have to do is engage your environment, hold the tension, and stay in the process.

Lesson 53

No Problem Can Be Solved Before its Time

Leaders don't like problems in their organizations; they want them to be pure and defect-free. They want their people producing at high levels and performing like a well-tuned machine. If problems do arise, they expect them to be discovered quickly and fixed right away. If they aren't, they get frustrated and take it out on their staff. Phrases like: "Bill should have seen this problem months ago. Doesn't he know what is going on in his group?" "This problem should have been fixed a long time ago. Why didn't Karen jump on it sooner and fix it?" can be heard coming out of leaders' offices.

This situation happens over and over. And why? Because of a simple truth: No problem can be solved before its time. **Problems hide until it's time for them to be noticed. No matter how vigilant we are, there are problems in our organizations that have yet to be discovered, yet business goes on.** When problems are identified, some of them are fixed right away. Others, however, show themselves slowly over weeks, month, or years. Solving them can take just as long. In these situations, problems need the environment to change before they can be discovered and fixed. It may be that the business has to shift focus for them to become a high enough priority, a new employee with the right skill set may need to be hired, or advancements in technology have to become available and implemented.

For years at Systemation, we have been struggling with entering contact data for workshop participants and getting completion certificates to them in a timely manner. It seems like a simple process, but it had been an issue of quality and timeliness for years. The evaluations we received from participants—which were required before they received their certificates—were hard to read due to varying handwriting abilities. The person responsible for data entry had other responsibilities that were becoming much more demanding. Lastly, completion certificates often did not reach the participants because of internal mail at the companies the certificates were sent to, along with distribution problems.

At some point, the problem reached the right time to be resolved in full. Trainers began traveling with iPads and workshop participants started entering their names and email addresses into them. After the workshops ended, the data was sent to our internal systems, which generate an email message to each participant, allowing them to go online and evaluate the workshop. After submitting the evaluation, the participant receives a pdf of their completion certificate. Problem fixed, but not before its time.

What does this mean for your organization? First, you have to shift your focus from how many problems you have to how much better you're becoming every time one is identified and fixed. Otherwise, you'll drive yourself crazy and put those around you in a constant state of fear. Shifting focus moves the organization away from identifying blame and toward rewarding others for helping the organization improve. It will make a huge difference in the way your staff handles problems. I'm not saying to be less investigative; I'm saying become a little more accepting of the problem identification and resolution process. It's like a fine wine. No problem can be solved before its time.

Lesson 54

You Can't Manage a Project While Working in it

N o person starts his or her career in the role of project manager. Project managers usually have spent years as members of project teams, contributing directly to the end product. As they gained experience and mastered their skills in many areas, they one day got the chance to manage a project. If they didn't crash and burn too badly, they got another chance, and so on.

Managing a project involves a totally different time and space perspective than just being a member on a project team. Team members are concerned with days and weeks in the future; a project manager's time horizon is months and years. Team members focus on ground-level details, while project managers have to take in the 30,000-foot, "big picture" view. Plus, formal project management activities involve much more coordinating and leading than producing.

But today, very few project managers have the luxury of spending all their time actually managing their projects. Most project managers are also responsible for work within their projects (requirements definition, design, development, etc.). Resource constraints and the proliferation of smaller projects are driving this change. This situation is very difficult because it forces the project manager to shift back and forth between *working in* his project and *working on* his project. Not only are these two worlds very different, the immediacy of work in the project weighs on the manager and often pushes out time for managing the project. And, the less time a project manager has to manage his project, the less chance he has of staying on course. If a project manager doesn't have time to manage a project in a certain week, it won't affect him then, but it will the following week, month, or quarter. It will sneak up on the project manager like a python snake and strangle him.

Reid, for example, found this out when he was working on an e-commerce project that was chugging along just fine. As it moved into the design phase, he got more involved in its day-to-day creation because his designers were struggling with the complexity of the requirements, which was something he enjoyed. As a result, he didn't spend enough time managing the project. After several weeks, he got a call from the IT sourcing company that was to provide his project database resources. They told him they were getting thin on them and needed a firm number of database development contractors ASAP. Reid went back to his resource projections and adjusted them based on the design. He needed two more people than he first estimated but found out he could not get any extras after calling back the sourcing company.

Reid had experience in database development, so he thought he could keep the project on track with extra work on weekends. After several more weeks, he was overwhelmed and had neglected his project management duties. He was walking by his director's office one afternoon, and she stopped Reid to inform him that she wanted a status report by the end of the week since she had not received an update in weeks. Reid spent the next two days collecting status information from team members and revising estimates. It turned out that a few of his team members who were supposed to be giving him half of their time each week on his project had only been giving him a few hours. As a result, his project was now going to be almost two months late. Needless to say, his director was very disappointed when she received the report.

To prevent yourself from getting into a similar situation, you have to strike the right balance between working *in* your project and working *on* it.

The first thing you need to do is set rigid boundaries on your time allocations. Every project is different when it comes to the amount of time required to manage the project effectively. So, set aside the first days of the week as the time you work on your project and manage it. When you feel as though you have tended to all the major areas of the project, then you can work in it. Do not waver here. The immediacy will creep in if you do. Also, the more you have to shift back and forth between working in and on your project, the less effective you'll be.

Next, make sure you review and address the needs in these four major areas of your project:

1. **Communication:** All avenues of communication from the team members up to you and from you to your project stakeholders. Are outside entities getting the information they need and are they keeping you aware of their situations?

2. **Team:** The emotional state of your team, including stress levels, morale, and personal issues. Are there any performance issues with any of your team members? Do they have all the tools needed to make their jobs easier?

3. **Schedule:** Embracing the reality of where you are and influencing future work to meet baseline expectations. Do you need to change the schedule to establish new expectations?

4. **Relationships:** All levels of stakeholders and resource providers within and outside your organization. Do you need to invest time into any critical relationships?

It's not ideal but it is what it is. Project managers have to live in two different worlds: working in a project and working on it. To keep yourself sane and successful, make sure you keep the two worlds as far apart as possible and live in each of them appropriately.

Lesson 55

So, You Can't Get People to Use the Software Tool

Y ou hear about it all the time: Organizations invest in a software tool and then struggle with its adoption. It could be project management, customer relationship management (CRM), requirements management, or any other type of software tool. What started with high hopes of efficiency and value ends up being a cost burden. But, there are four steps you can take to avoid this.

Focus on the Process

The problem is that the software tool became the focus and the overall process was ignored. Tools have lots of "gee whiz" features that put a sparkle in everyone's eyes, but the core purpose of the features in relationship to the process is often vague. So, before you begin to select a software tool, make sure the primary focus is on the process.

This process needs to be developed, refined, and documented, making sure it's a pure process. That is, it should be true to its intent, serve only that function, and demand the least amount of effort while providing the most value. The tool must integrate with and enhance the process.

Prepare Users

In most cases, users' first impressions of a new software tool are negative because it requires change and adds details to their world that they would rather not have to deal with. There's nothing directly in it for the users and they have little vision for how it will help the organization. In reality, this may not be entirely true but it's a common user perception.

To prepare users for the tool, provide them with the big picture and how the overall process helps the organization. Then, show them how the tool fits into the process and improves it. Finally, properly train the users and give them job aids to assist them in using the tool. But, keep in mind that none of this will be a success if you don't address the process items described above.

Identify Key Metrics

Most software tools are databases with lots of functionality that allow users to view and manipulate the data. Because of this, there are lots of metrics related to the process that can be collected. Collecting metrics that signify progress toward the end results of the process is crucial; however, identifying them out of all the available data is a challenge. You need to keep the big picture in mind while you look for the key data points. These data points will tell you if you're progressing through the process as designed, letting you know when there is and is not compliance with the process.

Let's say you have a good project management process in place. The intent of the process is to deliver products on time, within budget, and with all the requested functionality. You have selected your project management software tool and now need to identify the key metrics. The tool was selected because it has the capability to automatically calculate the project's major milestones. Some examples of data points that tell you the process is moving toward the end result could be:

- The number of tasks that don't have a predecessor or successor task in the network diagram;
- The number of tasks that have start dates in the past; or
- The number of tasks with fixed start dates that the software tool cannot adjust automatically, invalidating the overall schedule.

The more tasks of these types that you have, the more likely the project manager isn't complying with the process and its conventions.

Reports that contain the key metrics for the process should be easily produced and generated at a frequency consistent with the rhythm of the process. Some processes produce results on an hourly basis and some monthly. The frequency of the reporting period should be frequent enough for you to identify compliance trends and address them when they're fresh in users' minds.

Encourage Correct Behavior

Knowing when the process is or is not being followed as designed is great; correcting the behavior when it's not is the end goal. To correct behavior, the right level of management must be involved from the start. The manager needs to have responsibility over the process and the people. They alone have the capability to influence the user base's behavior. In addition, the success of the process needs to be very important to the manager. If it isn't, then the organization should never consider integrating a tool.

Also, don't try and get full compliance right from the start. Pick the most important areas of the process and concentrate on those first. Change is hard and takes time. You can always add areas as compliance increases.

Software tools are great but not the "be all." Start with the process and keep it top of mind. It will keep the tool in check and make sure it does what you want it to do, and not vice versa. Only then will it add value and gain the acceptance of your organization.

Lesson 56

Momentum: The X Factor in Project Success

In physics, momentum is a term used to describe a mass in motion. In competition, it's used to indicate which side has the upper hand. It's what aids a baseball team in winning the game by scoring five runs in the 9th inning with two outs. It gives the offense the edge in scoring the winning touchdown by moving the football the length of the field in six plays with only 26 seconds left. It makes for very exciting entertainment.

What most people don't know is that momentum is also a factor in helping project teams deliver successfully by boosting the performance of all team members. This is nowhere near as exciting as the sporting events described above, but it's momentum just the same.

Project momentum is like a small vehicle a team is pushing over rolling terrain. The amount of effort they put into pushing the vehicle, and the slope of the terrain, affects the vehicle's momentum. With real projects, every event, issue, action, and situation contributes to a project's momentum. They either increase or decrease it.

To take advantage of a project's momentum, project leaders need to do three things:

1. **They must become students of its behavior and benefits.**
   Project events happen. A mixed bag of positive and negative

events leaves momentum unchanged. A series of positive events substantially increases it, and conversely, a series of negative events substantially decreases it. A project's momentum also directly affects every project team member. When a project is on a good roll, it helps team members deal with small obstacles and disappointing events with greater ease. It also fosters stronger teamwork and individual performance. Progress comes with ease, as does success. When a project's momentum is down, project teams struggle to produce. They become disillusioned and attack each other over their lack of contribution.

2. **They must become sensitive to their project's related circumstances.** As I said earlier, every event, issue, action, and situation contributes to a project's momentum. Recognizing and analyzing these things is crucial to anticipating the effects it will have on momentum. Leaders must also be aware of their projects' current level of momentum and how it affects their team members. They can do this by evaluating their team's cohesiveness and individual behaviors.

3. **They must be the driving force in managing it.** No one person can have more impact on a project's momentum than the project leader because his or her attitude rubs off on individual team members. When momentum is rising, the project leader can boost it by highlighting the good fortune and its individual contributors. When momentum is falling, the leaders must be patient and look for signs of a turnaround for the better and become the team cheerleader. Leaders alone have the ability to rally the team to achieve a major milestone or not let the team fall into a deep hole when things are going bad.

You don't have to be a physicist to understand momentum. You also don't have to be a professional athlete to affect it. All you need to be is a conscientious leader to get the benefits from momentum.

Remember, it's not the big things that make you a success; it's the small things when they're all added up.

Lesson 57

What You Don't Understand Always Seems Simple

M ost people have many opinions on the way things *should* be. They ask questions like, "Why can't it be like this?" "Why aren't we able to do that?" "Can't they deliver it to me like this?" It's a great thing to ask questions, and everyone has an opinion. In fact, this kind of thinking is what makes the world better. It pushes us to change, try new things, and improve. But there's a fine line between asking questions and assuming the change is easy to accomplish.

At work, we observe salespeople who don't understand the difficulties with technology limitations. Yet, technology people are bewildered as to why salespeople struggle selling technologically superior products. Customers wonder why products aren't customizable to their exact likings, and customer service people are at a loss to understand why customers don't follow directions. All good stuff to consider.

But when the conversation turns to asking "How tough can it really be?", a line has been crossed. Wanting something different is one thing, passing judgment on how easy it is to accomplish is another. It moves from a simple want to an evaluation of a person's or organization's capabilities, and, it's usually based on little fact or understanding. This is the classic case of *what you don't understand always seems simpler than it really is.*

When your wants and assumptions are directed toward things outside your sphere of influence, then no harm, no foul. But when you do the same thing inside your sphere of influence, where your opinions carry weight, you can hurt others, make them defensive and put them in a difficult position. You can do all of this with little to no true understanding of the situation, limitations, or capabilities. It's not fair and not right.

A better way to move your desires closer to becoming a reality is to be open-minded and ask questions about what you don't understand. **If, after you have asked for something different and are told it's not possible, make it known you really don't know anything about the environment or situation but would love to learn more about it.** This will give you the opportunity to make sure your wants are understood, and to clarify anything that doesn't align with the other person's understanding. It also gives you the opportunity to brainstorm about what it would take to make what you want happen. By doing this, you become a partner and not a pesky opponent. It may not result in you getting what you want, but it will put you top of mind if there is ever an opportunity to make it happen.

Lesson 58

Drama Belongs in TV Shows, Not Organizations

TV shows that have lots of drama are very popular. People get hooked on the characters and their overly dramatic behavior. The drama is woven into story lines, adding many surprises and cliff-hangers to the plot of the show, bringing people back week after week.

But while drama is good for TV shows, it's not so good for organizations. It tends to waste people's time, weaken relationships, and diminish employee morale. Getting work done and completing projects on time is hard enough when individuals are focused, but it becomes downright impossible when drama steals people's attention and time.

We all know drama is basically taking something small or unimportant and making it bigger than it is. This behavior tends to play out through people in three different ways: overly sensationalizing **problems, habitual opposition** to ideas, and **sharing secrets.** Let's look at these in detail.

Problems

Problems become overly sensationalized when people first intensify the shock of encountering a problem. Phrases like "Did you hear what happened?" and "Can you believe it?" often accompany this phase of the drama. Then they move on to finding the people who were at fault. This is where good detective work comes into play. Lots of people have to be talked to, and multiple perspectives have to be considered. Then, in the final phase, the character of the individuals at fault is attacked. It's not hard to see how detrimental this is to organizations. Lots of energy is wasted, individuals get beat up, and reputations are destroyed.

Habitual Opposition

Habitual opposition is much harder to identify. A major symptom of this type of drama is when people leave meetings worn out as though they just went through three rounds in a boxing ring, but accomplished very little. It takes a long time to see this trend, but people who do this are basically playing tug of war with ideas and opinions. If someone presents their idea, then this person will take a counter view and question the validity of the other person's idea. Then they will argue against the idea as long as they can until they feel they have won. While organizations need opposing views to flesh out the best ideas, they don't need to waste time arguing for arguing sake. This only makes being at work a not-so-fun experience.

Sharing Secrets

The last type of dramatic behavior, sharing secrets, doesn't seem like drama, but that's because it's covert in its nature. In fact, another name for it is *covert gossip*. It always starts with the person saying "I'm going to tell you something but you have to promise not to tell anyone else." What follows is privileged information not about them but someone else. Plus, it most likely has been shared with others in the organization. This creates a buzz that everyone is aware of but can't talk openly about with each other. It undermines trust and relationships.

Drama exists to some degree in all organizations and it can't be ignored with the hope that it will go away on its own. Management has to recognize it, identify a strategy to confront it, and exert energy toward reducing it.

Some of the strategies for confronting drama require management action; others require educating employees. Here are three tried and true strategies for dealing with these types of dramatic behavior:

1. **For problems that get overly sensationalized, management needs to focus first on what needs to be done to correct the problem, then take steps to resolve it.** They then must focus not on who was at fault but on what caused the problem and how to avoid it in the future. Making statements like "It's not great that this happened but at least we know we're getting better because we experienced it and now know how to not let it happen in the future" will go a long way to show employees that it's counterproductive to lay blame on anyone.

2. **To combat habitual opposition, learn to stop playing tug of war over ideas or opinions.** When you experience this kind of behavior from someone, let go of the rope, so to speak, by saying "I disagree" and nothing more. It doesn't give the other person anything to react to or the ability to continue the argument. Another statement to try is "I don't understand what you're saying. Can you tell me more?" This makes them work much harder to keep the argument going.

3. **Lastly, when someone comes to you and says "I'm going to tell you something but you have to promise not to tell**

anyone else," tell them you'll promise to not tell anyone only if what they are about to say involves them and no one else. Otherwise, you don't want know what they want to tell you.

Once these strategies are in place, you'll see a significant decrease in the level of drama in your organization and an increase in productivity. If people want drama in their lives, tell them to watch more TV. Drama's not fit for organizational life.

Lesson 59

Use Metrics to Diagnose Your Project's Ills

N obody likes dealing with a sick project, but we've all been there and done that. Some projects start out sick and stay that way for the duration; others look healthy but then collapse near the end. Most of the time we guess the reasons for our project schedule's ills, hoping we're somewhat right, but still find ourselves at a loss for how to heal the project and hit the mark.

Diagnosing a sick project is not as mysterious as you might think. But it takes attention and discipline. Every project plan is built on a set of assumptions; some are out of the ordinary and documented in the project plan. These are the assumptions most of us call attention to and manage. Then there are the ever-present assumptions we don't give much attention to or announce. These are part of every project, so highlighting them would not enhance the usefulness of the project plan. Even though these assumptions are a part of every project, it doesn't diminish the importance of paying attention to them.

There are four assumptions that must be managed to ensure your project schedule stays healthy. These assumptions are that **the project scope is well known by all team members, people's estimates are good, work is sequenced properly,** and **the percentage of time each team member commits to the project is being fulfilled**. You can see that these assumptions are present on every project and aren't

217

worth putting in the project plan every time. Although, to manage them, you need to track a set of metrics continuously. Tracking these metrics means setting a baseline when planning the project, collecting data points weekly, and comparing the collected data to the baseline data to get variances.

The metrics are:

1. **Project's Completion:** the date the project is to be completed.
2. **Performance to Estimate:** the amount of effort (hours) to complete individual tasks.
3. **Estimates at Completion:** the amount of effort (hours) to complete the project.
4. **Effort Spend Plan:** the amount of effort (hours) expended to date on the project.

You need all four metrics to indicate your project's health. You may think that all you need to know is whether your project is scheduled to finish when you said it would. But this is not true because while your project may be scheduled to finish as planned, it may still be sick based on other metrics that won't reveal themselves until later. Plus, finding out the root cause for a late project requires all four metrics.

Let's look at situations related to the four assumptions:

- You know your project scope is not well known when your Performance to Estimate and Effort Spend Plan are right on but your Estimate at Completion has grown and your Project Completion is late. This shows that more work is being performed to complete newly discovered scope, adding to your Estimate at Completion and making your project late.
- You know the percentage of work you expected from your team members is not being realized when your Estimate at Completion is right on, but your Effort Spend Plan is low and your Project Completion is late. The total amount of estimated work

is solid because your scope is known and your estimating is just as you had planned, but you're not getting the resources as planned.

- You know your estimates are poor when the Effort Spend Plan is right on, but your Estimate at Completion is up and your Project Completion is late. Bad estimating is driving up the amount of effort required to complete the project and, with the same amount of resources, the end date has to be slipping out.
- You know your sequencing is not right when your Project Completion, Estimate at Completion, and Performance to Estimate are right on but your Effort Spend Plan is low. The only way you could not be slipping your project's end date when you're not getting the resource you expected is that you're planning to complete work in parallel. Usually this is a fantasy view that won't become a reality.

With each situation, the more detailed you are in planning and recording your metrics, the more resolution you'll have related to the true root cause to your project schedule's ills. You have to balance this with the size of the project and your need for certainty on the project's completion data. It may not be worth the effort to be more detailed.

Don't get distressed if you don't fully understand the principles at work with the metrics and their associated assumptions. These are typically taught in advanced project management training courses. Knowing they exist can motivate you to learn more now or have them be of use to you later should the situation warrant them.

Lesson 60

Pruning and Growing Your Team

Most people in management are handed their teams when they're promoted or assigned a new organization. They get what they get but have the freedom to make the team their own. While this may seem like a finite process, the reality is that it's a never-ending one.

Statistics will tell you that some team members will be great performers, several good, and a few will be poor. That may be reliable news but it doesn't really matter when it comes to adopting a new team. It's not as simple as replacing all poor performers. Not all better-than-average employees are a good fit for all managers, and not all managers are a good fit for all better-than-average employees. When there's a change in management it's not necessarily the manager's responsibility to adjust to the employees even if the majority of them think he or she should. Sometimes managers need to replace top performers to make the team their own.

This is exactly what Dennis, for example, had to do when he was hired to replace the previous manager of a software development organization. The organization had a history of good performance and had a number of top performers, but was not embracing cutting-edge industry practices. Dennis was specifically hired to get the organization to adopt these practices and take it to the next level.

Dennis had a ton of experience managing organizations and was a thought leader in the industry. His management style was well suited to changing organizations and producing results. After six months on the job, several top performers confronted Dennis about his style and the changes he was initiating. They told him he needed to change if he wanted them to stay. Dennis told them he didn't think it was working between them either and it wasn't anything personal; it just wasn't a good fit between them and him. Dennis offered them severance packages to leave and they did. Because Dennis was a thought leader in the industry, he was able to recruit other top performers. A year later, he said his new employees were not any better than the ones that left but the new employees did enable the organization-wide transformation Dennis needed to be successful.

Even after you replace all the people you need to replace initially, you still won't have a final team. In fact, you never will. People change over time and so do job responsibilities. Nothing is static. Where there once was a perfect match between an employee and job responsibility, things can get out of sync when new skills are needed due to technology advancements. In addition, schedule flexibility can disappear when an employee's family situation changes (such as a new child), and job responsibilities can diminish as processes are streamlined.

This means employees, especially long-standing ones, must be constantly evaluated to see if they still fit culturally and are producing the value they're being compensated for. As soon as the trajectory of an employee's value contribution begins to flatten out and the trend of their compensation continues to climb, tough conversations need to take place. Also, it's worth the chance to look at trading up on marginal performers. Usually, you have to kiss a lot of frogs before you find a prince and, as you know, each time you go through the cycle of hire/evaluate/keep or fire, it takes a substantial amount of time and effort. Yes, it causes disruption but it also makes sure your team doesn't get complacent or stale. It's the manager's responsibility to set the pace and tone at work even if it makes them uncomfortable.

Finding replacements for your team, or hiring in a time of growth is not simple. Managers never want just a warm body to fill a position; they want a top performer. They can identify who they think is a top performer, but having that prediction come to pass is different. Here again, you may have to kiss several frogs before you find the right person. It can be a hard process to stay engaged in, but it's a must if you want to end up with top performers.

Managing your team of unique individuals is a huge responsibility, but a crucial one. They are the ones who ultimately produce your organization's value. Getting the best team together is good for everyone no matter how hard it is or how long it takes. It's a living organism that needs to be pruned in order to grow.

Lesson 61

Are You an Intentional Leader?

Most leaders would answer that question with a solid "yes." That's because they judge their level of thought, analysis, and response to any given situation to be thorough, deliberate, and undeterred. But if you were to send out a 360-degree evaluation to their employees, the responses that come back may tell another story. Regardless of how intentional leaders think they are, it's their employees who truly know them.

The way people engage you in the workplace is based on their perception of your intentionality. People working in organizations with unintentional leaders are cynical about why their leaders want something done. Closure is not valued in the organization and the work quality suffers as a result. Negativity and avoidance dominate the work environment.

On the flip side, intentional leaders have a lot of credibility related to "why" they want something done and if it's worth doing. Work in this type of organization is completed as requested and its intended results are apparent. The work environment is positive and engaging.

Intentionality is all about time and effort. It means learning what you need to know to plot a good course, make a decision, or take action. It also means being aware of the volume and pace of work within your organizations in relation to other priorities, staying the course, and seeing things to the end.

Being intentional is not a true/false thing; it's a continuum. Your intentionality varies as your behavior varies during different efforts, such as:

Effort	Time-Frame
Requests	Days
Projects	Months
Initiatives	1-3 Years
Strategies	3-5 Years

It's far easier for a leader to be intentional on requests with their employees because it only involves days to initiate, monitor, and complete them. There is minimal time and effort involved. Being intentional in strategy, however, is a lot harder as the amount of time and effort to learn what you need to know to plot a good course, be aware of the volume and pace of work, and stay the course is far greater. So, a leader can be more intentional when the time frames are smaller, less so when they're longer. Leaders need to be intentional across the continuum.

As I stated earlier, the best way to identify how intentional you are as a leader is to observe how employees engage you related to work. Let's look at each context timeframe and the signs your employees may give you to indicate whether or not you're being perceived as intentional.

Requests

Not intentional: The more time employees put between your request and its fulfillment, the greater the chance you'll forget about it. They may say when you remind them of the request that they were just about to do it but, in reality, they'll avoid you until you forget about it.

Intentional: Employees either complete the request or tell you they'll get it done by a certain date without you having to remind them.

Projects

Not intentional: Project delays are measured in half-lifes, like radioactive materials. The end deliverables are completed haphazardly without attention to detail. Employees just want to close the project out and move on to anything else.

Intentional: Regular status is delivered by employees and reviewed together. There's a lot of attention paid to the end deliverable to make sure it hits the mark.

Initiatives

Not intentional: Initiatives are like gases. In the right environment they take on a liquid form that employees can grasp, but without attention they become vapor and vanish into the air, never to be seen or heard from again. Employees show excitement in the beginning but wander off when the leader no longer pays attention.

Intentional: No matter how long the initiative lasts, employees can clearly articulate the future state and its benefit to the organization. Employees enjoy looking back and seeing the transformation and evolution of their collective efforts.

Strategies

Not intentional: These don't exist and are never discussed by employees within the organization. Work life is a series of non-related events that must be carried out without a higher purpose.

Intentional: It's hard for employees to completely connect with a strategy. It may be too broad or sophisticated, but when the leader brings it up time and time again, employees slowly start to connect with it.

It takes focus, discipline, and dedication to be intentional. Not everyone has these traits, and as a result, struggles to be intentional. If you're in this situation, try partnering with a peer in your company and leverage their strengths in these areas to help you compensate for your weaknesses. It doesn't need to be on a day-to-day basis; monthly can help immensely. Also, avoid getting too busy and overwhelmed; it's a natural precursor to intentionality.

If you're feeling like you want to take some risk and you're ready for straight feedback, create an assessment out of the above text and ask your employees to rate you on a scale (such as, 1 to 5) for each time frame. The feedback may hurt a little, but your employees will be glad you asked and will be ready to support you more in the future.

Lesson 62

All Projects Bring about Change

By their nature, all projects induce change on individuals. It may be a change in process, product line, job aids, tools, organizational structure, personnel, or at the least, expectations. As you know, not everyone deals with change the same way. Also, change can be halted or derailed because of the way people respond to it.

That means a project's success has as much to do with managing change as it does producing an end product. Project managers and business analysts do not always realize this because they're so familiar with the change and have been processing it for so long that they minimize the impact it will have on others. When change impact is minimized, it's not planned for and individuals going through the change tend to resist and fight back.

Even though each of us deals with change differently, all of us go through the same process of accepting it. We first want to know why the current state needs to be changed. Then we want to know what the future state will be like. Lastly, we want to know how we're going to be transitioned from the current state to the future state.

While this information helps us move through the change process, our emotional response to the information can hinder acceptance. Experts tell us that when we process a change, we experience, to some degree, seven different emotions: immobilization, denial, anger, bargaining, depression, exploration, and acceptance.

With projects, time is on our side when it comes to change. We always know when the change will occur, and if we're smart, we'll start planning for it right after we complete the planning for the project. There are a number of strategies and tools at our disposal to help people move through the change process and experience the varying emotions:

Communication

Communication is the most powerful change tool. Getting information out early and often is best. Repetition, with alterations in wording and tone, ensures the information is embraced. Breaking the transition into smaller steps helps people move toward acceptance. Legitimizing people's anger and not taking it personally can take a very uncomfortable emotion and dissolve it.

Learning

Learning must be provided when the change requires people to do things differently. Make sure they know what resources are available to them. People going through change need to know they will be prepared for it in advance of when they will be required to perform differently.

Rewards

Lastly, there is no better way to motivate someone to experience change than to offer them rewards for embracing it. The rewards need to be consistent with the degree of change and resistance that may be expressed. The rewards also need to be enjoyed as close as possible to the time when resistance may be at its highest level. Offering someone a reward in the future for putting their resistance aside now is not going to work for most people.

The level of effort required to address project change can vary greatly. Putting in more than what's needed does not make sense and is a waste. Most likely, project managers and business analysts will not succumb to this. If they make an error, it will be on the side of not putting in enough effort. That's what we want to avoid.

Lesson 63

Why Culture Trumps Your Organization's Proclamations

All organizations have grand visions of how they want to be seen. It always involves customers, employees, and the organization as a whole. They want customers to feel appreciated and completely satisfied with the level of customer service they receive. They want employees who are empowered to take initiative and add value in everything they do, and they want to be seen as an organization that's admired for its innovation and treatment of employees. Organizations proclaim these things in mission and value statements, speeches, press releases, articles, proposals to customers, and a variety of other media.

What organizations say and document is what they want. What others observe is often much different. This is because culture always trumps proclamations. Culture is like dark matter in our universe. Scientists can't see or touch it, but they know it's present because their current mathematical models for the universe do not fully explain what they observe. Something big is missing: an X factor, dark matter. When an organization's proclamations do not reflect what is observed, it's because of their X factor, their culture. It dictates employee behavior when they're being watched and when they're left alone. It's the single most powerful influence in an organization.

A poor culture corrupts an organization into having customers who feel they're a nuisance and subservient to standard policy, employees who put in only enough time to look busy and don't dare do anything other than what they're told, and organizations that cling to the status quo and care solely about boosting their bottom lines.

Exactly how does this happen? It happens one experience at a time. An employee is shamed or disciplined for trying something new and failing. Project celebrations are eliminated to save money even though profits are at a record high. Customers with unique situations are rammed through the standard customer service process. It's these raindrops that, over time, create a river that wears down the mountain side.

Culture is created at the top and driven down through the organization. Even if senior management doesn't intentionally create a culture, one gets created anyway. It's just something that happens in groups of people. Cultures are created one way or another.

To intentionally create a culture; identify six pillars you want to establish as core tenets of your organization. You can start with your proclamations, which I'm sure were well thought out. Then, steer your organization toward those pillars by:

- Hiring, firing, encouraging, and disciplining employees based on your six pillars.
- Being careful when making decisions because you may erode what you're trying to build up. Dive into the systemic cause-and-effect relationships to ensure decisions move you closer to where you want to be.
- Constantly modeling the behavior that supports the culture you want and make sure your subordinates do the same. (They'll pass it down to the rest of the organization.)
- Staying with it; it takes time.

Also, keep in mind that subcultures can exist within larger cultures. While their influence cannot deviate too far from the larger cultures, they can still be different. This gives managers leeway in their departments. Even if their larger organization's culture is causing unwanted behavior, managers are still able to put some of it in check by creating a strong subculture. (Example: If a company culture does not value workers' families, a manager can still set up special dinners with families to show he values them.) No manager is totally helpless.

Lastly, every person in an organization has the choice to be influenced by the culture or not. If it's a good culture the choice is easy. If the culture is toxic, then it's a much more difficult choice, one that could affect their future employment and peer relationships. Even though the influence of a culture is very powerful, everyone still has a choice and the responsibility for that choice.

So, next time you hear an organization's leaders proclaiming who they are, remember the proof is in the pudding. Watch and see: Your observations will reveal their culture and the driving force behind employees' decisions and behavior.

Lesson 64

Never Care More about Your Project than Your Sponsor Does

It's no secret that project managers don't hold all the authority that's required to keep a project on the right path during its lifespan. They need sponsors to, at times, approve more resources or time, cast the final vote on a split decision, limit end users' sprawling needs, and participate in resolving lots of unforeseen issues.

Sponsors will always say they're committed to the project's success and, in their minds, they mean it. However, during the life of a project, their actions may say otherwise. It's mostly true that they're committed to the project, but their other commitments may take a higher priority. They care, but not as much as they care about other things.

As a result, project managers find themselves in situations in which their sponsors are unavailable. If the sponsor is available, then they may not make decisions quickly enough. If they do make decisions, they may not be well thought out and go in a direction the project manager doesn't recommend.

Project managers who find themselves in these situations can get very frustrated. They're committed to the project's success and know the sponsor is hurting their project. Because they care so much, they often choose to overstep their bounds and take actions to keep the project on the right path. This leads to project managers doing things without telling their sponsors as well as keeping information from them. These are telltale signs that a project manager cares *more than the sponsor.*

So, is it bad for a project manager to care more about a project than the sponsor does? Well, there's no black-or-white answer to this question that accommodates all situations. The real question project managers should be asking is: "When I care too much, will my actions put me in a more difficult situation than if I had stayed within my bounds and let the natural consequences fall as they may?" The answer will most often be "yes." By caring more than their sponsors, project managers risk harming the relationship, being held liable for making decisions they don't have authority to make, and being devious by withholding information.

Take Rachael, for example. She had been a project manager for years and had a very good track record at delivering results. This was the first time she worked with Devon as the project sponsor. As usual, the project started off well but soon ran into a few issues that Rachael needed Devon to help resolve. Rachael had a very difficult time getting Devon to engage the issues and help resolve them. Devon was habitually unresponsive and, after a while Rachel's frustrations hit a peak. She began to rely on her experience to get things done without Devon's involvement. She felt justified in doing this because she didn't want an unsuccessful project to taint her reputation. Most of the decisions Rachael made were solid, but one came back to haunt her. She did her best to keep the situation hidden by making sure Devon was kept out of the loop, only to see the situation explode, attracting Devon's attention. When he became aware of the situation, he asked question after probing question that painted a clear picture of how much Rachael kept him in the dark and worked around him. Rachael was forced off the project and had to be transferred to another department once management was briefed.

Now that we know what caring too much looks like, let's look what caring *just enough* entails. The first thing project managers need to do is work on obtaining the right mindset. They're in a no-win situation and have to believe that they stand a much better chance of success by staying within their bounds by not assuming their sponsors' authority. Also, success will come from staying in the light and avoiding the dark when information is withheld from a sponsor. In fact, providing the sponsor with an overabundance of information is actually best. Lastly, project managers should not attempt to coerce their sponsors into getting involved, taking action, or taking the action the project manager wants. In extreme cases, this will annoy a sponsor and could cause them to become even further removed from the project. As I stated earlier, this is a no-win situation. By taking these steps the project will be impacted if the sponsor chooses to not get involved and take appropriate action. Here again, having the correct mindset helps deal with this situation. A project manager is better off with this course of action than they would be if they cared too much and went underground.

Matching a project manager's level of caring to their sponsor's is not easy. It's all about the way the project manager makes sense of it. This view may be extremely counterintuitive to the way project managers have operated and gotten ahead in the past. That's OK. Even if they just become more aware and observant of the pitfalls of caring too much, they'll be better off. The aim here is to help project managers stay off the path of deceit—and possible unemployment.

Lesson 65

Four Keys to Building Strong Work Relationships

Most work environments require interacting with others. Some people view these interactions as separate events they must endure, while others view them as enriching, ongoing relationships. The truth is, you get out of your work relationships what you put into them. If you're totally independent in your work environment, not requiring anything from anyone, then you don't need to read any further. But, if you depend on others, you need to learn how to build strong work relationships.

There are four key behavior traits that contribute to building strong relationships. You need to be **trustworthy, care about the other person, be committed to excellence in your performance**, and **bond through adventure**. Let's look at each of these in more detail.

1) Be Trustworthy

It's important for you to do what you say. When you commit to something, others listen, and then watch. They want to know if you can be trusted to deliver on your commitment or if you'll just blow it off. When you deliver something, will you deliver it as requested and on time? Or will it be incomplete or late?

Others also want to know if you're going to attempt personal gain at their expense. They'll watch how you go about getting things you want, looking for methods or actions that take advantage of others. Even if they're not involved, it will be a telltale sign that they need to watch their backs when they work with you.

2) Care about Them

People want to know if you care about them as people, or see them as objects, a means to an end. No one wants to be viewed as a resource for someone else's consumption. They want to be known as unique individuals with life experiences, emotions, and as having choices in their work demands. Showing someone you care about them requires showing respect regardless of their positions in the company and gaining general knowledge of who they are and what they like and dislike.

In practice, this means scheduling a meeting or conversation instead of just dropping in or calling. If you can't schedule in advance, don't interrupt an ongoing conversation. Politely wait, then ask if it's a good time to chat. Before you discuss any business, ask them about their personal life. When you're first building the relationship, ask general questions about their past and current experiences. Topics could include family, hobbies, vacations, pets, past jobs, etc. As time goes on, you can ask more specifics questions, but wait until you sense trust developing between the two of you.

Another way to show you care is to reflect back the information you receive. If Sally tells you she has a big vacation starting tomorrow, then make sure you ask her about it the next time you see her. If Bill tells you his dog died, don't forget about it, then ask him if he took his dog to the park two weeks later.

3) Commit to Excellence

Very few people like to work with low performers. You can't help but get a little slimed from someone else's deficiencies and poor results. Working with a person like this can require twice the effort and time of a competent worker. This is why your work attitude and quality affect your work relationships. Committing to excellence means showing initiative and not waiting for someone else to point work out to you. Having a can-do attitude signals you're not afraid of a challenge and that you'll carry your weight when times get tough. Remember to be thorough and complete when you declare something finished. This will not only make you pleasant to work with, but it will also inspire others to follow your commitment to excellence.

4) Bond through Adventure

Adventures are not all good or all bad; they're a mixture of both. In a work environment they're always experienced with a group of people, and have a general beginning and end. Adventures never kill us or take us to nirvana, and they usually have a central theme. In our personal lives, adventures may be vacations, kids sports teams, neighborhoods, community efforts, etc. In work environments, they may be projects, departments in transition, recessions, building moves, working with a very difficult person, etc. Adventures almost always develop deeper bonds because they're shared experiences that we get to survive together, laugh and cry about, reminisce about, and to some extent relive the emotions again.

The key to reaping the benefits of bonding through adventure is by creating adventures in your day-to-day work environment. This starts with identifying the themes of your group adventures, highlighting the highs and lows you experience, acknowledging that things will change and the adventure will end, and enforcing the group experience of it.

Each of these key behaviors requires multiple interactions over time to make a difference. There is no pill you can take to instantly have strong work relationships. In the beginning, 10 good interactions may take you a level deeper in your work relationship with someone, but one bad one will set you back a level. Over time, grace becomes more a part of your relationships and good and bad interactions become less pivotal to the strength of a relationship. Strong work relationships will not only make you more productive, they'll make you a lot happier too.

Lesson 66

Putting Purpose into Your Organization's Efforts

It's no secret that individuals and teams produce better results when they're motivated. Managers, coaches, and parents often search far and wide to find a source of motivation for those they desire better results from. Motivation can come in the form of a benefit or purpose. Benefits are usually finite and have shorter life spans; whereas, purpose can last a lifetime.

In companies, providing a sense of purpose is the best motivator. The purpose can come from what a product or service provides to customers and the benefit derived from it. Purpose can also come from the positive change or end result a project will produce when completed. These are great motivators to employees and drive them to be the best they can be.

However, even these items aren't a guarantee when it comes to providing employees a sense of purpose. In large companies, the products, services, and customers can be very distant. Take, for example, an auto parts manufacturer that makes parts for a car line, which is assembled by one of the major automakers. They can be several times removed, which significantly reduces their impact on an employee's sense of purpose. Projects are also limited since they don't always have a compelling purpose and are temporal, meaning they don't last forever.

There's one surefire way to provide all employees a long-term sense of purpose: Identify all the ways your organization provides value to your customers, define each employee's link in the value chain, and promote each individual's contribution to the value chain. This value chain is ever present and requires contributions from every employee in the organization to succeed. If an employee can't connect to it, maybe they shouldn't be in the organization. Also, it doesn't matter if the customer is the ultimate external customer or an internal customer.

Let's look at the details of making this happen:

- **Identify all the ways your organization provides value to your customers.** There are many ways and means by which your organization touches your customer: the products and services you provide them, interactions you have with them, and all the different ways they observe your organization. Each of these touch points is an opportunity for your organization to provide value. During this process, you may identify other places where you should be adding value and things you're doing now that you should stop doing.
- **Define each employee's link in the value chain.** Each link in the value chain is a role one or more employees perform. There can be many employees who contribute to the value chain through one role, and there can be one employee who contributes to the value chain through many roles. For each role, define the link by giving it a short, one-sentence description. The description needs to be in the context of the value your organization provides its customers. For instance, instead of the description "Answers phones," use "Connects people with people." Make it meaningful in the context of value. Then, list the high-level responsibilities of that role and future opportunities for increasing that role's value contribution. Lastly, indicate if it's a direct or support role. Direct roles deal with

the customer directly while support roles aid someone within your organization so they can connect better with the customer directly.

- **Promote each individual's contribution to the value chain.** Nothing beats the consistency of messaging to ingrain a way of thinking into someone's day-to-day work life. Leaders need to perpetually refer to the value their organizations provide and each individual's contribution to it. This practice will establish within all employees the purpose and motivation to be the best they can be.

Some of you are thinking that this is a gimmick and that you can derive your own sense of purpose, motivating yourself to greater achievement. Great! That's you. If you're a leader, you can't afford to rely on each individual to come up with their own purpose because, if it doesn't work, you'll be left with an underperforming organization that you judge to be full of bad eggs. In the end, however, others will judge you as the underperformer for your lack of leadership. Seek and follow the value chain; it will lead to success.

Lesson 67

What's the Profile of a Good Project Manager?

M anagement often wishes it had a very clear mechanism for identifying candidates who will turn out to be better-than-average project managers. They know that having to rely on their gut works fairly well but still feel there must be a better way to evaluate candidates in order to succeed more often.

For more than a decade, Systemation has evaluated project managers using its comprehensive Project Manager Assessment. The overwhelming majority of project managers we assessed were part of a larger training and coaching program in which a Systemation coach mentored each project manager for two hours, every other week, for six months. Because of this, Systemation became intimately aware of the project managers' strengths and weaknesses in performance and was able to reflect back on the assessment results and draw specific conclusions.

Before we discuss these findings, you need to know some background information. The assessment has three distinct categories: knowledge, skills, and aptitudes. The knowledge portion identifies, through multiple-choice questions, the amount of PMBOK (Project Management Body of Knowledge) the project manager comprehends. The skills component targets the softer skills and assesses them using an evaluation tool given to everyone involved in the project. Lastly, the aptitudes evaluate the core characteristics of the individual project manager through a battery of psychological tests. Before we received the results, it was clear that the knowledge and skills categories would improve over the course of the Systemation program, but aptitudes were core to the individual and could not be easily changed without a major environmental change and five to 10 years of time. Given that, Systemation was not sure what trends would develop in the years to come related to aptitudes and the ultimate profile for a good project manager.

Hundreds of assessments later, the profile for a good project manager looks like this:

People-Oriented

Good project managers must be people-oriented. They must enjoy interacting with people, recognize emotions in others, and empathize with others. Less than 14% of the people chosen to go through the assessment scored low on their people orientation. All of those who did score low in this aptitude struggled significantly in building relationships and in getting the most out of their teams; they ultimately had to be reassigned to other positions. The lesson here is that people orientation is the most important aptitude in project managers, and those who select from project manager candidates usually have a good feel for the presence of this aptitude too.

Centered

The next aptitude in importance is how centered a project manager is. Project managers are centered when they're confident, aware of their own assets and liabilities, their desire to achieve, their ability to remain calm in stressful conditions, and flex when plans don't go as expected. If their score was moderate to high, as it was for 81%, their performance was not negatively impacted by this aptitude. If the score was low, they tended to be seen as emotionally volatile and not safe for their team members to get behind and follow. If this aptitude is not strong enough, it can undermine a project manager's other strengths to the point that they too cannot remain in project management positions.

One of the biggest surprises was the remaining four aptitudes (big picture-oriented, creative, systematic, and detail-oriented) had a distinct correlation. Let's look at each of these before we dive into the correlation.

Big Picture-Oriented and Creative

Big picture oriented is when one sees the future in high resolution, keeps a vigilant focus on the project's goal, and acquires the appropriate level of perspective in order to comprehend the whole. Creative project managers think in ways outside the norm and identify multiple solutions to problems. Every project manager scored high or low in *both* of these areas in the same survey. This makes sense since they both come from the right side of the brain. Project managers who scored low in these areas tended to struggle with comprehending the project as a whole, seeing the over-the-horizon consequences, and coming up with solutions to maneuver the project to keep it on track.

Systematic and Detail-Oriented

Project managers who are systematic are organized and structured in their approach to work and accept regimented consistency for the sake of efficiency. Those who are detail-oriented focus on the here and now and strive for breadth, completeness, and correctness at the lowest level of detail. Here again, each project manager scored high or low in both of these areas, which come from the left side of the brain. If project managers score low in these areas, they don't consistently acquire detailed status reports from project team members, they don't put in the time to re-forecast regularly with precision, and they generally become disconnected from the current state of the project.

The surprising correlation is that project managers either scored **high in big picture-oriented and creative** and **low in systematic and detail-oriented, or vice versa.** Ultimately, this data resulted in the identification of specific strengths and weaknesses in good project managers. No more than 3% of the project managers assessed scored low on all four aptitudes.

Only 6 % of the project managers evaluated scored high on all six aptitudes. All remained project managers for only 18 to 24 months before they moved on to the next rung of the corporate ladder. They were stellar project managers and excellent in all facets of the discipline.

If you look at the spectrum of poor to excellent project mangers, very few who are considered candidates for project management positions will fail, the vast majority will meet the profile of a good project manager, and very few will be stellar. From this data, **management has to realize that their chance of finding a top-notch project manager and having them around for some time is remote. They have a far greater chance of finding a good project manager who will have a specific set of weaknesses that can be identified and helped using some coping mechanisms.** It's not the ideal dream management envisions, but at least it's a reality that can be managed.

Lesson 68

Stop Seeking a Work-Life Balance

S ince the late '70s people have been struggling with the work-life balance issue: the balance between an individual's work and personal life. A lot has been written on this subject, trying to give men and women alike a strategy to balance work and personal demands. The problem is: **Achieving a balance is impossible.**

In the past, there were physical boundaries between our work and personal lives that helped keep them separate. The struggle with balance came down to the amount of time spent at each location. Today, technology has removed the physical boundaries and allowed work activities to infiltrate personal time and personal activities to infiltrate work time. Computers and mobile devices are as central to our lives personally as they are for our work.

We all have a disposition toward work and personal activities. You've heard the saying that some people "live to work" and others "work to live." There's a continuum between the two views and each of us has a place on it. This disposition is not assigned to us; we choose it. It drives us to choose our profession, employer, and priorities.

The time demands for work and personal activities aren't consistent from day to day, month to month, or year to year. Our work and personal lives have seasons. At work, we have busy and slow times of the year. Projects have critical deadlines that must be met and new phases that give us a little break. The business climate can bring about budget cuts that require us to do more with less, as well as good times that allow us to pursue new opportunities.

In our personal lives, we have significant life events like weddings, the births of loved ones, and times we must take care of aging parents and attend funerals. Our kids require a different level of support when they're adolescents than they do when they leave home and live on their own. How we unplug on vacations can mean a week crammed with adventure or sitting quietly on a deck in the mountains.

Also, most employers don't care if you find a balance. They make it easier for you to do work during personal time, while making it harder to engage in personal activities during work time. They care only about the *seasons* of work – busy times and slow times—not those that give way to more personal time.

With all of this thrown into the pot, you can see how impossible it is to balance our work and personal lives. A better goal is to pursue an ebb-and-flow between the two. At any one time, the mix between work and personal activities can be significantly out of whack, but you have to envision a point in time when things will swing the other way.

It requires discipline and an understanding of the consequences for letting your disposition toward work and personal activities lead you. Those who "live to work" struggle to keep work in check and tend to not take enough time for family, friends, and self. Those who "work to live" struggle to meet the challenge of work activities and end up with fewer rewards and opportunities than those of their co-workers.

It also requires paying attention to the signals around you. If you've been paying attention to work activities for too long, you'll start to dislike what you do, and those close to you will let you know you've been absent. If you've been paying attention too long to personal activities, your supervisor will let you know and you'll become disgruntled with your employer's view of your performance.

There's no silver bullet to feeling good about the mix of time you engage in work and personal activities. But, at least you now understand what forces are at play that can put you in this uncomfortable predicament. You're the only one who can change it. Thankfully, you know the seasons will change and you can choose a time in the future to be different.

Lesson 69

The Chicken or the Egg:
Is it the Same for Leaders and Followers?

Y ou've heard the saying. Which came first: the chicken or the egg? It's used to highlight a circular reference between two entities, such as leaders and followers. Leaders need followers to get better *organizational* results, while followers need leaders to get better *individual* results. It makes sense. However, this view is not as common as it should be. More specifically, it's not a dominating belief among leaders.

Some mature leaders and a greater majority of new leaders have a different view of the symbiotic relationship between leaders and followers. It goes like this: **Leaders have unique skills and strong past-performance records. Followers can't do things as well as leaders. Thus, leaders are more valuable than followers.**

Let's look at an example of a leader and a follower:

Eric is the manager of a small department responsible for the development and support of a software application. He was out sick one week and when he returned the following Monday he got briefed on a situation his department encountered in his absence. Leslie, a customer service representative, received a call from an irate customer, complaining that the capability she just upgraded was not working properly. Leslie wanted to get the problem fixed right away because the customer's company is one of their biggest users. She went to Jerry, who was responsible for fixing application bugs, and the two of them worked out a solution. By the end of the week, the fix was in place and the customer was happy.

Upon hearing about this, Eric almost blew a gasket. The department was planning to release a new version of the application in six weeks that would change the way the customer interacts with it. The fix Jerry and Leslie worked on to help the customer would just create a bigger problem for them once the new version was released. Eric went to his office and began a dialog with himself that went like this: Leslie was in the last new release meeting and heard what was going on. Why didn't she ask the customer more questions to understand how they were using the application? Why didn't Jerry ask the development team about how the capability would change in the new release? Also, why had no one in his department told the customer about the new release when they asked for the upgraded capability? Why can't these people connect the dots? I never made these kinds of mistakes. Sometimes I think I would be better off without them.

Let's go back to the train of thought that drives Eric's beliefs.

- **Leaders have unique skills and strong past-performance records.** This is true. Leaders start off as followers and, over time, develop a unique set of skills and a track record of good performance that launches them into leadership roles.
- **Followers can't do things as well as leaders can.** This is both true and false. Followers can't do a leader's job as well as a leader can. Yeah, so what? Followers are not supposed to be good at what leaders do. They're supposed to be good followers, and at this, they can be just as good if not better than leaders. Leaders must not expect followers to behave and perform just like them. If they did, then everyone would be a leader and there would be no followers to get the work done.

Leaders should expect followers to behave and perform just like followers and nothing more.

- **Leaders are more valuable than followers.** This is false. Yes, there are fewer leaders than followers. Leaders are compensated more than followers and leaders have authority over followers. None of this implies a greater value. There are fewer leaders than followers because you need only one leader for a group of followers. Leaders are compensated more than followers because they have much more responsibility. They oversee all the followers' efforts. If you were to add up the followers' compensation, the leader's compensation would be a fraction of the total. Leaders have authority over followers because, with responsibility, there's a need for authority to make it work. Followers are just as valuable as leaders.

To create a healthy relationship with followers, leaders must expect followers to think and behave just like followers. They must create an environment and look for ways to help followers be the best they can be. They must value followers more than themselves. In Eric's case, he needs to accept that his followers are thinking and behaving like followers and not expect them to think and behave like *him*. Eric then needs to realize that his followers can collectively get more done and produce greater results than he ever could by himself. This frees him to not focus so much of his energy on how to change the way followers think and behave, but more on how he can change their environment with process and job aids to get the results he's looking for.

If leaders choose to stay with the unhealthy way of thinking about the leader-follower relationship, they can expect a negative impact on their organization. Followers will sense they're being harshly judged and undervalued, causing them to feel resentment and bitterness. Their performance can't help but be tainted by it.

Conversely, when followers have a great leader, they don't need to be convinced to follow. It's natural for them to do so since they want to produce their best for their leader. It's a leader's choice. Choose wisely and be a great one.

Lesson 70

When Nice Users Drive You Nuts

You know and appreciate them, those super nice people who are always cordial, very amenable, and never demanding or burdensome. In group settings, you hardly know they're around. When you interact with them one on one, it's always a pleasure. The conversation stays very positive and noncontroversial. In most settings, you wish the world had a lot more people just like them.

But there's one situation in which you wish they were different; when they're users and you need them to articulate what they dislike and want in a product.

Business analysts are trained to analyze the current state and develop a future state based on feedback from users. The larger the user base that participates in defining the future state, the better the end product will be. Users who tend to be critical and demanding are good to have in this situation. They have no problem telling you what they don't like and lots of ideas when it comes to what they want. Information flows abundantly from these types of users.

This is not the case with "nice" users. The current system is always just fine and they can't think of anything they would change. You hear them but you don't fully believe them. You've heard rumors of unique side processes they use that assist them in getting their work done using the current product.

Then, there's the lack of desired feedback that comes when a business analyst proposes a change to the current product. Everything that's proposed to the "nice" users is just fine. They can make it work just as it is. This is most certainly true, but as a business analyst your job is to make things more efficient, not just workable.

The best way to get good information out of "nice" users when it comes to criticizing the current state of a product is to **sit next to them and watch them use it**. Record the things they do outside of the product (examples: recording an order number so they can refer to it later, or calculating a discount based on an amount to verify from a different screen) they would never think to tell you about since they do not associate them with the product. This type of evaluation may be time consuming, but if you can identify a few "nice" users, do it without overburdening your schedule. Through observation and questions you can identify what workarounds they use and the areas of the product they get frustrated with.

The best way to get good information out of "nice" users when asking for feedback on a future state of a product is to offer them two approaches to a feature and ask them to pick the one they like best. Then, ask them why. When you ask "nice" uses what they would change about a future state product, they automatically assume their desires are not worth the effort it would take to change things. When you ask them to decide between two different approaches it takes their perceived value of their desires out of the equation. Now, they're only deciding between two items. Getting them to tell you why they like one over the other is valuable information.

There's a good chance you have more "nice" users than critical and demanding ones. It's easy to rely on the latter for your user input, but it may not be the consensus if you were to get good information out of the "nice" users. As a business analyst, you need to put in the extra effort to ensure the future state will be most useful and efficient. Don't worry about offending them; after all, they're "nice," remember?

Conclusion

W e all know it's important to learn and grow at work so that we perform better in our roles and responsibilities. When we first began our careers all we did was learn. We had very little work experience and needed to learn the basics of how to work in our new professions. Learning never stopped for us as we experienced many situations that forced us to refine our skills because feedback on our performance was readily available and immediate.

After many years of work we became masters at our jobs and found ourselves only getting better as we experienced new situations and interacted with our peers. Now, learning only comes through infrequent experiences and reflection with our peers. The experiences are always present as work-life never stands still, yet reflecting on them is both optional and a must for learning. Reflection requires us to stop, review, analyze, and draw conclusions. It's not extremely hard to do, but it takes discipline to step away from day-to-day activities and cycle through the recent experiences to glean some lessons learned.

Organizational leaders have a more difficult learning challenge than others. Their experiences involve the "big picture" perspective and systematic thinking. Feedback on their performance is not immediate or readily available. As a result, their reflection needs more time and seclusion to tweeze the lessons learned and needed adjustments.

This book came about through many leaders' experiences and reflections in a number of project- based organizations. Leading these types of organizations, whether you're new to it or an old pro, is a challenge. Very few experiences are exactly the same, and the breadth of your responsibilities related to your people, projects, and organization can feel overwhelming.

Systemation hopes you're able to shorten the learning curve through the lessons we gained over the years and documented in this book. We're sure you related to many of the topics. Our hope is that you take some time to reflect on why you related so much to them and look for ways to do things differently.

CPSIA information can be obtained at www.ICGtesting.com
Printed in the USA
BVOW040246290312

286118BV00002B/2/P